Washington Bucket List Adventure Guide

Explore 100 Offbeat Destinations You Must Visit!

Craig Baker

Canyon Press
canyon@purplelink.org

Please consider writing a review!
Just visit: purplelink.org/review

ISBN: 978-1-957590-00-4

FREE BONUS

Discover 31 Incredible Places You Can
Visit Next! Just Go to:

purplelink.org/travel

Table of Contents

Friday Harbor

Glacier

Gold Bar

Grand Coulee

Hansville

Hoodsport

Ilwaco

Issaquah

La Conner

Leavenworth

Sedro-Woolley

Sequim

Skykomish

Snohomish

Snoqualmie

Spokane

How to Use This Book

Welcome to your very own adventure guide to exploring the many wonders of the state of Washington. Not only does this book offer the most wonderful places to visit and sights to see in the vast state, but it provides GPS coordinates for Google Maps to make exploring that much easier.

Adventure Guide
Sorted by region, this guide offers over 100 amazing wonders found in Washington for you to see and explore. They can be visited in any order and this book will help you keep track of where you've been and where to look forward to going next. Each section describes the area or place, what to look for, how to get there, and what you may need to bring along.

GPS Coordinates
As you can imagine, not all of the locations in this book have a physical address. Fortunately, some of our listed wonders are either located within a National Park or Reserve, or near a city, town, or place of business. For those that are not associated with a specific location, it is easiest to map it using GPS coordinates.

Luckily, Google has a system of codes that converts the coordinates into pin-drop locations that Google Maps can interpret and navigate.

Each adventure in this guide includes GPS coordinates along with a physical address whenever it is available.

It is important that you are prepared for poor cell signals. It is recommended that you route your location and ensure that the directions are accessible offline. Depending on your device and the distance of some locations, you may need to travel with a backup battery source.

About the State

Washington is simply overflowing with natural wonders to visit. The federal government owns more than one-fourth of the state's land, with the National Park Service owning three national parks and five national forests. The Washington State Park System boasts over 100 state parks. This abundance of well-preserved nature helps to make Washington one of the greatest destinations in the world for hikers, mountain climbers, and all other types of outdoor enthusiasts. You'll find nearly 700 miles of hiking trails crisscrossing Washington's state parks alone.

There are five active volcanoes in the state: Mount Baker, Mount Rainier, Glacier Peak, Mount Adams, and Mount St. Helens. Washington is also the most glaciated state in the contiguous United States—just Mount Rainier has roughly 25 glaciers. Washington is home to nearly *8,000* lakes as well, which are perfect for fishing, boating, and other water sports.

The Giant Octopus

One of the great legends of Puget Sound is that of King Octopus. Many believe that the biggest octopus in existence lives under the Tacoma Narrows Bridge. For generations, locals have told tales of the 600-pound octopus—some fear that the monster attacks deep-sea divers, while others think the aquatic monarch just wants to be left alone.

There is some truth to this legend. The largest species of octopus in existence is the giant Pacific octopus, and this species does live in Puget Sound. However, giant Pacific octopuses only live for three to five years, and the largest giant Pacific octopus on record weighed 156 pounds. They are beautiful creatures, though, and very intelligent. They can also change color and alter their texture to blend in with plants, coral, and rocks.

Fun Fact: Mount Olympus got its name in 1788 when Captain John Meares, a British fur trader, wrote of the peak, "If that not be the home wherein dwell the gods, it is beautiful enough to be, and I, therefore, call it Mount Olympus."

Landscape and Climate

Washington has earned its nickname as the "Evergreen State" with its many forests full of spruce, fir, and cedar trees that cover roughly half of the state's land. Located in the Pacific Northwest, the state has a varied and dynamic landscape. The Cascade Mountains are full of lush green hillsides, glistening glaciers, beautiful meadows, scenic lakes, and jewel-blue rivers. Many of the peaks and slopes remain snow covered all year long. There is also plentiful wildlife. One might find bobcats, cougars, martens, marmots, bears, deer, elk, and even moose in the wilderness of the Cascades.

The land in Western Washington is hilly and mountainous, thanks to the glaciers of the last ice age. That same glacial activity produced the many islands along the Puget Sound. The Olympic Peninsula features rain forests, alpine peaks, legendary waterfalls, and glacier-carved lakes. In the rainforests, you will find giant ferns, blooming orchids, and Sitka spruce trees up to 300 feet tall.

Eastern Washington is mainly made up of mountains and farmland, but large portions of the landscape give way to strange rock land formations and barren bedrock. This desert was formed by a series of ice-age floods and is full of tall, dry waterfalls and deep ravines.

The Cascade Mountains divide Washington into two very different halves. Western Washington is often called the "wet side" of Washington, while Eastern Washington is the "dry side." Western Washington has mild temperatures and is generally wet during all the seasons except summer, though snow is rare. Meanwhile, the deserts and grasslands of the east are much drier with more dramatically high and low temperatures in the summer and winter, respectively.

Deception Pass State Park

Out of all of Washington's state parks, Deception Pass is the most popular. With gorgeous views, shadowy coves, old-growth forests, rugged cliffs, abundant wildlife, and an iconic high bridge, it's not hard to see why.

This park offers something for everyone. Cranberry Lake is a great spot for swimming and fishing, making it perfect for families.

There's plenty of Puget Sound beachfront for relaxing and searching for seashells. It's not unusual to see a family of seals or even a whale.

You can also enjoy Rosario Beach's tide pools and boating at Cornet Bay. For hikers, there are several forests and bluffs to traverse. The park is home to Hoypus Forest, one of the state's few remaining old-growth forests.

Best Time to Visit: June through September

Closest City or Town: Anacortes

Physical Address: 41020 State Rte 20, Oak Harbor, WA 98277

GPS Coordinates: 48.3930° N, 122.6473° W

Did You Know? Names like *Rosario Beach* and *Fidalgo Island* date back to 1792 when Spanish Captain Salvador Fidalgo explored the area.

Alta Vista Trail

The Alta Vista Trail is a 1.5-mile loop hiking trail located in Mount Rainier National Park. It is known for its spectacular wildflower fields in the summer and its dramatic, sweeping views of Mount Rainier. The trail is extremely popular in the summer, and both the upper and lower parking lots at the trailheads fill up quickly. While the Alta Vista Trail itself is fairly easy, there are several opportunities to connect to other trails about halfway through the hike. The trail is mostly paved, although there are points where it becomes rough or narrow. Be sure to stay on the marked path so that you don't damage the fragile ecosystem in the area.

Best Time to Visit: Visit during the week in the spring or fall to avoid crowds.

Pass/Permit/Fees: While there is no fee to visit the Alta Vista Trail, there is a $15-per-person fee or a $30-per-vehicle fee to visit Mount Rainier National Park.

Closest City or Town: Ashford

Physical Address: 39000 State Route 706 E, Ashford, WA 98304

GPS Coordinates: 46.7892° N, 121.7370° W

Did You Know? In 1897, James Skinner established a tent camp in the area of the Alta Vista Trail. It was eventually purchased by John Reese and became known as "Reese's Camp" or "Camp of the Clouds." In 1889, John B. Hartman, a climber out of Tacoma, provided the trail with the name Alta Vista, meaning "high view" in Spanish.

Mount Rainier

When you think of mountains in Washington, Mount Rainier is likely the first one that comes to mind. At 14,410 feet above sea level, this mighty mountain has earned its fame. The active volcano is the most glaciated peak in the lower 48 states.

Here, you'll find vibrant wildflowers around the snow-topped volcano while ancient forests blanket its lower slopes.

There are over 260 miles of hiking trails to enjoy at Mount Rainier National Park.

These trails will lead you through subalpine meadows, river valleys, and old-growth forests. You'll wander amongst picturesque lakes, rivers, and streams while exploring the glaciers.

Best Time to Visit: July and August are the best months for wildflowers. To avoid the crowds, try a spring or fall visit.

Closest City or Town: Ashford

Physical Address: 39000 State Route 706 E, Ashford, WA 98304

GPS Coordinates: 46.7859° N, 121.7368° W

Did You Know? The last time Mount Rainier erupted was about 1,000 years ago.

Myrtle Falls

Mount Rainier is gorgeous on its own, but when you add in the spectacular beauty of Myrtle Falls, you're truly in paradise. The 72-foot-tall waterfall is one of the state's most photographed locations. With Mount Rainier as its backdrop, almost anyone can get a professional picture of the pristine waters and stunning mountainside.

The hike to the falls is easy, making it a great place to visit for people of all ages and abilities. The waterfall drops into a deep gorge carved over millions of years by Edith Creek, which eventually winds its way to Paradise Valley. The horsetail-style falls run all year but can be inaccessible during the winter if there's snow on the trail.

Best Time to Visit: The best time to visit Myrtle Falls is during the summer as the area may be inaccessible in the winter.

Pass/Permit/Fees: While there is no fee to visit Myrtle Falls, there is a $15-per-person fee or a $30-per-vehicle fee to visit Mount Rainier National Park.

Closest City or Town: Ashford

Physical Address: 39000 State Route 706 E, Ashford, WA 98304

GPS Coordinates: 46.7919° N, 121.7323° W

Did You Know? A former Mount Rainier guide named Myrtle Falls in 1907 after a woman he met while guiding a tour through Mount Rainier National Park.

Silver Falls

This impressive waterfall is the culmination of the Silver Falls Loop, a 2.7-mile hiking trail in Mount Rainier National Park. Silver Falls tumbles over several ledges before plunging 40 feet into a pool of deep blue water. While you can quickly get to the falls from SR-123, the better way to experience the breathtaking waterfall is by hiking the Silver Falls Loop that begins at the Ohanapecosh Visitor Center. On your way to the waterfall, you can read a few interpretative signs that explain the history of the area, including the one-time existence of the Ohanapecosh Hot Springs, which developed into a commercial tent camp resort by 1921. Plans for a full-service resort were scrapped when Mount Rainier National Park was expanded to include the hot springs in 1931.

Best Time to Visit: Visit Silver Falls in the spring and summer when the water is running at its peak.

Pass/Permit/Fees: While there is no fee to visit Silver Falls, there is a $15-per-person fee or a $30-per-vehicle fee to visit Mount Rainier National Park.

Closest City or Town: Ashford

Physical Address: 39000 State Route 706 E, Ashford, WA 98304

GPS Coordinates: 46.7553° N, 121.5595° W

Did You Know? The word *Ohanapecosh* is the Upper Cowlitz Indian name that means "clear stream" or "deep blue," both of which perfectly describe the plunge pool at Silver Falls.

Spray Falls

This veiling horsetail–style 354-foot waterfall is one of the must-see falls in Washington. The trailhead begins at Mowich Lake in Mount Rainier National Park and passes through a picturesque forest, crosses over several sparkling streams, and ends with the awe-inspiring Spray Falls.

This towering waterfall is always impressive, but it's especially breathtaking in the spring when the snowmelt pushes the flow to its limit, causing the water to violently burst over the sheer rock face of the mountain. In fact, at certain points downstream, you'll even be able to feel the spray on your face, long before you ever see the actual waterfall.

Best Time to Visit: The best time to visit Spray Falls is during the spring when the water is running at its peak.

Pass/Permit/Fees: While there is no fee to visit Spray Falls, there is a $15-per-person fee or a $30-per-vehicle fee to visit Mount Rainier National Park.

Closest City or Town: Ashford

Physical Address: Spray Park Trail, Ashford, WA 98304

GPS Coordinates: 46.9174° N, 121.8419° W

Did You Know? For a longer hike, you can continue past Spray Falls onto the Spray Park Trail to travel the "Around Mother Mountain Hike." This 16-mile loop will take you through both Seattle Park and Spray Park.

Sunrise Visitor Center

The Sunrise Visitor Center is located at the highest point that is accessible by vehicle in Mount Rainier National Park. In the summer, it is surrounded by wildflower meadows, and on clear mornings, visitors are treated to spectacular sunrises that feature incredible views of Mount Rainier and Emmons Glacier. From the visitor center, you'll be able to see nearly 360 degrees in all directions, taking in views of the valleys, Mount Rainier, and other Cascade Range volcanoes like Mount Adams. The Sunrise Day Lodge, located near the visitor center, offers food and gifts in July, August, and September.

Best Time to Visit: The best time to visit Sunrise Visitor Center is during the summer, as Sunrise Road is closed in the winter.

Pass/Permit/Fees: There is no fee to visit Sunrise Visitor Center, but there is a $15-per-person fee or a $30-per-vehicle fee to visit Mount Rainier National Park.

Closest City or Town: Ashford

Physical Address: Sunrise Park Rd, Ashford, WA 98304

GPS Coordinates: 46.9152° N, 121.6437° W

Did You Know? There are numerous trailheads located at Sunrise Visitor Center, including the 1.5-mile Sunrise Nature Trail, the 1-mile Emmons Vista Overlooks Trail, the 3-mile Frozen Lake Loop Trail, the 2-mile Silver Forest Trail, the 3-mile Shadow Lake Loop, and more.

Tipsoo Lake

Located in Mount Rainier National Park, Tipsoo Lake is a popular spot for wildflower viewing in late July through mid-August. The best part about visiting Tipsoo Lake is that you don't have to be an expert hiker to reach the gorgeous wildflower meadows since the path around the lake is mostly flat and easy to follow. There is a longer hiking trail that begins at the lake and ascends about 700 feet to an overlook that provides spectacular views of Tipsoo Lake and Mount Rainier. The 3.5-mile Naches Peak Loop Trail offers even more wildflower meadows to see, and you'll likely catch glimpses of elk, deer, and marmots along the way as well.

Best Time to Visit: The best time to visit Tipsoo Lake is during the late summer and early fall when the wildflowers are in bloom.

Pass/Permit/Fees: There is no fee to visit Tipsoo Lake, but there is a $15-per-person fee or a $30-per-vehicle fee to visit Mount Rainier National Park.

Closest City or Town: Ashford

Physical Address: 39000 State Route 706 E, Ashford, WA 98304

GPS Coordinates: 46.8697° N, 121.5173° W

Did You Know? Swimming is not allowed at Tipsoo Lake, as it is a critical breeding ground for the Cascades frog and Western toad, which are sensitive to oils from human skin.

Baring Mountain

Baring Mountain's imposing north face is one of the most dramatic sights in the Central Cascades. The north face is one of the great sheer mountain walls in the U.S., comparable to those in Yosemite.

The mountain is known for a variety of difficult climbing routes that provide spectacular views of the Central Cascades and adjacent valleys. This might not be the best peak for an easy climb, but it sure will give you a great workout!

Less experienced climbers and hikers can enjoy the beauty of Barclay Lake at the base of Baring Mountain. The sight of the mountain's striking northern face from this vantage point simply can't be beaten.

You can stroll or sit by the lake and admire the gorgeous view. The Baring Lake hiking trail is a little over 2 miles, making it perfect for kids.

Best Time to Visit: April to October is best for hiking and nature trips. The summer months are ideal for climbing.

Closest City or Town: Baring

Physical Address: Barclay Lake Trailhead is found at NF-6024, Gold Bar, WA 98251

GPS Coordinates: 47.7925° N, -121.4593° W

Did You Know? Baring Mountain is the third-steepest peak in Washington.

Bellevue Arts Museum

The Bellevue Arts Museum, locally referred to as "BAM," was born out of the first Pacific Northwest Arts and Crafts Fair held in 1947. The outdoor fair's success led to the creation of the Pacific Northwest Arts and Crafts Association, which would eventually develop the Belleview Art Museum in 1975.

It was originally housed in a former schoolhouse, then in a funeral home, and then on the third floor of the Bellevue Square shopping center before finding a permanent home in downtown Bellevue in 2001.

In 2005, the name changed to Bellevue *Arts* Museum as the mission evolved to include draft and design in the museum's offerings.

Best Time to Visit: The Bellevue Arts Museum is open Wednesday through Sunday from 11:00 a.m. to 5:00 p.m.

Pass/Permit/Fees: Adult admission is $15. Seniors/students/military admission is $12, and youth ages 6 to 17 are $8. Children under the age of 6 are free.

Closest City or Town: Bellevue

Physical Address: 510 Bellevue Way NE, Bellevue, WA 98004

GPS Coordinates: 47.6161° N, 122.2011° W

Did You Know? The Bellevue Arts Museum has hosted the annual Bellevue Arts Museum Arts Fair for more than 70 years. It features over 300 national artists each year.

Bellevue Botanical Garden

In 1981, Bellevue citizens Cal and Harriet Shorts deeded their home and 7.5-acre lot to the City of Bellevue with the caveat that it remain a public space. Three years later, Iris and Bob Jewett conceived of developing a botanical garden on the property and launched the Bellevue Botanical Garden Society to fulfill their vision.

Incorporating the early twentieth-century Sharp Cabin (relocated from NE 8th and 124th Avenue NE) into the design, the Bellevue Botanical Garden partially opened in 1990 with the Perennial Border, the Yao Japanese Garden, and the Fuchsia Garden before fully opening in 1992. Eventually, the garden expanded to include the Dahlia Display, the Waterwise Garden, the Wildflower Garden, the Alpine Rock Garden, the Native Plant Garden, Rhododendron Glen, the Ravine Experience, and additional features.

Best Time to Visit: The Bellevue Botanical Garden is open daily from dawn to dusk, but late spring and early summer are the best times to see flowers in bloom.

Pass/Permit/Fees: There is no fee to visit the Bellevue Botanical Garden.

Closest City or Town: Bellevue

Physical Address: 12001 Main St, Bellevue, WA 98005

GPS Coordinates: 47.6093° N, 122.1787° W

Did You Know? Bellevue Botanical Garden now encompasses a total of 53 acres!

Bellevue Downtown Park

The Bellevue Downtown Park is a 21-acre park located in the center of Belleview. It features a 0.5-mile promenade, a 240-foot-wide waterfall, a reflecting pond, 10 acres of open lawn space, formal gardens, the Inspiration Playground, and more than 120 donated benches that have been purchased by Belleview residents through the Donation Bench Program. Public art, numerous paved walking paths, and a World War I Memorial are all additional amenities in the park. The primary purpose of this park, which was completed in 1990, is to be a passive and unstructured-use park in the middle of a bustling downtown area that can provide a "respite from the activities of busy urban life."

Best Time to Visit: The best time to visit the Bellevue Downtown Park is during the warmer weather of spring, summer, and fall.

Pass/Permit/Fees: There is no fee to visit the Bellevue Downtown Park.

Closest City or Town: Bellevue

Physical Address: 10201 NE 4th St, Bellevue, WA 98004

GPS Coordinates: 47.6133° N, 122.2044° W

Did You Know? The Inspiration Playground is designed for children of all abilities to explore and play at their own speed. It features interactive equipment that offers an inclusive, engaging, and accommodating experience for children ages 2 through 12.

Bellevue Zip Tour

For the more adventurous visitors to Washington, the Bellevue Zip Tour will take you on a 35-mph journey that's 80 feet above the ground. On zip lines of up to 458 feet in length, you'll enjoy spectacular views of Mount Baker and Glacier Peak as you travel above a bigleaf maple tree forest. Choose from seven zip lines, cross two suspension bridges, and enjoy a safe, exhilarating adventure that will be the highlight of your trip.

You can also challenge yourself on the Bellevue Aerial Adventure challenge course, which provides 2.5 hours of physical challenges to test your agility, balance, and teamwork.

Best Time to Visit: The Bellevue Zip Tour is open daily from April through October from 9:00 a.m. to 5:00 p.m., but your actual zip-line tour must be scheduled.

Pass/Permit/Fees: Adult admission is $85, and children between the ages of 8 and 17 are $70.

Closest City or Town: Bellevue

Physical Address: 14509 SE Newport Way, Bellevue, WA 98006

GPS Coordinates: 47.5695° N, 122.1460° W

Did You Know? Bellevue Zip Tour has been open since 2006. It was developed as part of a partnership between Northwest Teambuilding and the City of Bellevue to expand youth services in the region.

Chism Beach Park

This waterfront park is located on the shores of Lake Washington and features a picnic area, a fishing dock, a swimming beach with seasonal lifeguards on duty, a children's play area, and a boat launch for non-motorized watercraft. While on the smaller side, this 18-acre park is beautifully landscaped and ideal for gatherings like weddings, parties, and other celebrations.

Watercraft is only allowed near the beach during the non-swimming season. The views from the park are ideal for watching the sunset, and several walking trails begin in the park and lead through the nearby neighborhoods.

Best Time to Visit: The best time to visit Chism Beach Park for swimming is during the summer. For taking a watercraft out on the lake, the best time to visit is during the fall or spring.

Pass/Permit/Fees: There is no fee to visit Chism Beach Park.

Closest City or Town: Bellevue

Physical Address: 1175 96th Ave NE, Bellevue, WA 98004

GPS Coordinates: 47.6006° N, 122.2106° W

Did You Know? On a clear day, you'll be able to look across Lake Washington from Chism Beach Park and see Seattle.

KidsQuest Children's Museum

The KidsQuest Children's Museum is an interactive facility that focuses on learning through play. It emphasizes the development of science, technology, engineering, art, and math (STEAM) skills through more than 25 exhibits specifically created for children up to the age of 10. There is also an outdoor space that is designed for construction and music.

Best Time to Visit: The KidsQuest Children's Museum is open Wednesday from 9:30 a.m. to 5:00 p.m., Thursday from 9:30 a.m. to 3:00 p.m., Friday from 9:30 a.m. to 6:00 p.m., Saturday from 9:30 a.m. to 7:00 p.m., and Sunday from 11:30 a.m. to 5:00 p.m.

Pass/Permit/Fees: Tickets for adults and children (ages 1+) are $10 each. Infants are free, and military members receive a discount of $2.

Closest City or Town: Bellevue

Physical Address: 1116 108th Ave NE, Bellevue, WA 98004

GPS Coordinates: 47.6216° N, 122.1959° W

Did You Know? Established in 2005, the museum is an award-winning creative play space for about 206,000 visitors each year.

Mercer Slough Nature Park

This 320-acre nature park is an urban refuge located in downtown Bellevue. It offers a peaceful environment for numerous outdoor activities, including canoeing, hiking, biking, and blueberry picking. The park is home to the largest remaining wetland around Lake Washington and contains hundreds of plant species, such as water lilies and wild irises, and water resources. More than 170 species of wildlife make their homes in the park, including beavers, otters, jays, blue herons, and bald eagles. More than 7 miles of trails, boardwalks, and paved paths wind their way through the park and connect to blueberry fields, a garden, greenhouses, and the historical Winters House.

Best Time to Visit: The best time to visit Mercer Slough Nature Park is during late spring or early summer, especially if you want to pick blueberries.

Pass/Permit/Fees: There is no fee to visit the Mercer Slough Nature Park, but individual activities may charge separate fees.

Closest City or Town: Bellevue

Physical Address: 2101 118th Ave SE, Bellevue, WA 98005

GPS Coordinates: 47.5939° N, 122.1840° W

Did You Know? Canoes and kayaks can be rented at Enatai Beach Park in the Mercer Slough Nature Park, or visitors can bring their own non-motorized watercraft and launch it from the free Sweyolocken Boat Launch.

Meydenbauer Bay Park

As the most recently updated beach park in Bellevue, Meydenbauer Bay Park is notable for its play area, beach house, whaling building, pedestrian pier, viewing terrace, and outdoor classroom. Originally, between the 1890s and 1921, this park was the landing site for ferries that shuttled passengers between Seattle and Bellevue. It was also once the location of Wildwood Park, a popular dance hall for Seattle residents. In 1953, it became Bellevue's first park.

Currently, there are several paved and unpaved trails throughout the area, featuring native plants and trees and a fishing dock that's open to the public. Kayaks, canoes, and stand-up paddleboards can be rented from the boathouse, or visitors can bring their own people-powered watercraft.

Best Time to Visit: The best time to visit Meydenbauer Bay Park is between late June and Labor Day when there is a lifeguard on duty.

Pass/Permit/Fees: There is no fee to visit Meydenbauer Bay Park, but individual activities may charge separate fees.

Closest City or Town: Bellevue

Physical Address: 419 98th Ave NE, Bellevue, WA 98004

GPS Coordinates: 47.6126° N, 122.2112° W

Did You Know? Until 2019, when the renovated park reopened with an expanded beach section and the 420-foot-long pedestrian pier, Meydenbauer Bay Park was known as Meydenbauer Beach Park.

Meydenbauer Center

The Meydenbauer Center is Bellevue's convention facility that hosts more than 250 events each year. Established more than a quarter of a century ago, the center welcomes approximately 150,000 guests on an annual basis and has served more than 5 million people since its inception. It's home to the Meydenbauer Center Theatre, the only professional performing arts theatre in the city.

The center features performances from symphonies, bands, comedians, and more. In addition to the 410-seat performing arts theatre, three meeting rooms encompass 2,500 square feet, and there is a 36,000-square-foot carpeted space for conventions, galas, presentations, concerts, trade shows, and more.

Best Time to Visit: The best time to visit the Meydenbauer Center is when there is a show or event in town that you want to attend. See the website for dates and times.

Pass/Permit/Fees: The fee to visit the Meydenbauer Center is based on the show or event you attend.

Closest City or Town: Bellevue

Physical Address: 11100 NE 6th St, Bellevue, WA 98004

GPS Coordinates: 47.6166° N, 122.1918° W

Did You Know? In a single week, the Meydenbauer Center Theatre can feature up to 212 performers on its single stage.

Larrabee State Park

Larrabee State Park was Washington's very first state park. The camping park is known for its picturesque views of the San Juan Islands and Samish Bay. This park has several fantastic recreation options—you can go paddling, diving, and fishing. The freshwater Lost and Fragrance lakes provide wonderful trout fishing. The park is also a prime location for shellfish harvesting.

There are plenty of scenic spots throughout the park that are perfect for spending time with family or getting lost in solitary thought. Though the shore is the main draw of this park, hikers won't be disappointed. Larrabee State Park features a Douglas fir and salal forest full of hiking and mountain biking trails.

Best Time to Visit: The park is open year round, but the shore is best enjoyed during the summer months.

Required Items: For information on camping reservations, as well as passes and permits, refer to the Washington State Parks website.

Closest City or Town: Bellingham

Physical Address: 245 Chuckanut Dr, Bellingham, WA 98229

GPS Coordinates: 48.6552° N, 122.4914° W

Did You Know? The Larrabee family donated 20 acres to the state in 1915 so that the land could be made into a park. The park was named after Charles Xavier Larrabee and opened to the public in 1923.

Whatcom Falls Park

Whatcom Falls Park is a 241-acre park in the Bellingham area that has more than 5 miles of trails that take hikers through forests and meadows and provide spectacular views of a deep-creek gorge and still ponds. Located 100 yards from the parking lot, you'll see a gorgeous moss-covered stone bridge that has stood for 100 years that will take you to the main falls. The falls can be reached in just 15 minutes, but there's plenty of other attractions to explore as you walk through the forests and meadows. Several trails in Whatcom Falls Park connect to other parks, making Whatcom Falls Park an excellent trailhead for a day-hiking trip. There is also a second waterfall on the west side of the park called Whirlpool Falls.

Best Time to Visit: The best time to visit Whatcom Falls Park is during the spring or summer after heavy rain.

Pass/Permit/Fees: There is no fee to visit Whatcom Falls Park.

Closest City or Town: Bellingham

Physical Address: 1401 Electric Ave, Bellingham, WA 98229

GPS Coordinates: 48.7512° N, 122.4271° W

Did You Know? Along with the falls and the stone bridge, Whatcom Falls Park has a fish hatchery, an off-leash dog area, multipurpose fields, an outdoor basketball court, a fishing derby pond, picnic tables and shelters, tennis courts, and playgrounds.

Mount St. Helens National Volcanic Monument

Also known as *Lawetlat'la* to the indigenous people of Washington state, Mount St. Helens is an active volcano that last experienced a major eruption in 1980, becoming the deadliest and costliest volcanic event in U.S. history. In total, 57 people died and 200 homes were destroyed, among other damage. The mountain is located in the Gifford Pinchot National Forest, and since the eruption, has been left to return to its natural state. It is one of the most popular climbing destinations in the state but may be closed for climbing depending on the recent volcanic activity.

Best Time to Visit: The most popular times to visit Mount St. Helens are during late spring and early fall.

Pass/Permit/Fees: A one-day pass to the park where Mount St. Helens is located costs $11.50 (including a transaction fee). There is also a climbing permit that costs $15 per person, per day. There is a limit on the number of climbers, so check the Gifford Pinchot National Forest website when planning your adventure.

Closest City or Town: Castle Rock

Physical Address: 3029 Spirit Lake Hwy, Castle Rock, WA 98611

GPS Coordinates: 46.2508° N, 122.1987° W

Did You Know? Mount St. Helens's English name is in honor of Lord St. Helens, a friend of George Vancouver, the first explorer to visit the area in the late 1700s.

Lake Chelan

Lake Chelan is a 50.5-mile lake that is popular with boaters, water skiers, windsurfers, sailors, and fishermen. There is 495 feet of dock for boats along the lake, with some near the launch and others near a lakeside camping area. You will need a launch permit or Discover Pass with a daily launch permit to put a boat in the water.

The lake is closely associated with the Chelan Native American tribe, which existed in the area before homesteader John W. Stevenson arrived in 1862 and a military post was established in 1880 by Colonel John Merriman. The state park that surrounds the lake opened to the public in 1943.

Best Time to Visit: The boat launch and all facilities are closed from November 1 to March 1 each year, so the best time to visit Lake Chelan is between March and October.

Pass/Permit/Fees: There is no fee to visit Lake Chelan, but a dock-fee permit is required.

Closest City or Town: Chelan

Physical Address: 7544 S Lakeshore Rd, Chelan, WA 98816

GPS Coordinates: 48.9099° N, 120.2020° W

Did You Know? Lake Chelan is the third-deepest lake at 388 feet below sea level. It's also the 26th deepest lake in the world.

Columbia Plateau Trail State Park

The 130-mile-long Columbia Plateau State Park Trail is a favorite of hikers and mountain bikers alike. There are 38 miles of hiking trails, another 38 miles of biking trails, and 34 miles of horse trails. The park offers views of rolling landscapes and wide-open skies above.

Passing the Turnbull National Wildlife Refuge, you'll encounter a whopping 200 species of birds, as well as elk, moose, deer, and small mammals. On the 23-mile Fish Lake trail, there will be breaks for rest and swimming.

At the southern boundary of the Columbia Plateau Trail, you can hike along the Snake River. There's a lower-grade hike that's much easier for beginners, and a higher-grade, rockier hike where you'll get to see remnants of an old rail line.

Best Time to Visit: Year round

Closest City or Town: Cheney

Physical Address: 19087-19099 S Cheney Spangle Rd, Cheney, WA 99004

GPS Coordinates: 47.5611° N, 117.5604° W

Did You Know? The Spokane, Portland and Seattle Railway Company constructed a rail bed in the Columbia Plateau Trail State Park area in the early 1900s, but the company never actually connected the line from Portland to Seattle. The line was eventually abandoned in 1987 and bought by Washington State Parks in 1991.

Snake River

Snake River is the Columbia River's largest tributary, originating in Yellowstone National Park. The river is home to the Pacific Northwest's biggest whitewater rapids and is a popular spot for river rafting.

Snake River flows through Hells Canyon, which is situated along the borders of Oregon, Washington, and Idaho. The mighty canyon is deeper than even the Grand Canyon. At Hells Canyon, there are many opportunities for water sports like jet boating and fishing, as well as hiking, hunting, and camping.

If you're in the mood for a gentle stroll along the river, the paved Greenbelt Walkway Trail is ideal. The trail begins at Granite Lake Park, then follows the Snake River for almost 7 miles to Chief Looking Glass Park in Asotin.

Best Time to Visit: The summer months are the best time for whitewater rafting.

Closest City or Town: Clarkston

Physical Address: Greenbelt Walkway, 338 10th St, Clarkston, WA 99403

GPS Coordinates: 46.3823° N, 117.0484° W

Did You Know? In 1805, Lewis and Clark famously traveled down the Snake River and reached the Columbia River on October 16. They initially called Snake River "Lewis's River" after Captain Lewis.

Steptoe Butte State Park

This 168-acre day-use park provides a breathtaking view of a lush green valley and soft, rolling hills from a butte that consists of some of the oldest rock in the Pacific Northwest. This butte marks the original North American continent's border and, at various times throughout history, has served as a wagon road, an observatory, and even a hotel site.

The Cashup Hotel, named for James "Cashup" Davis, who first summited the butte in 1880, opened its doors in 1888, but the location was determined to be too inconvenient. It closed in 1902 and was destroyed by fire in 1911, paving the way for the area to be donated for preservation purposes. The land later became part of Steptoe Butte State Park in 1946.

Best Time to Visit: The best time to visit Steptoe Butte State Park is in the summer when the weather is mild.

Pass/Permit/Fees: There is a $10-per-day fee to visit Steptoe Butte State Park.

Closest City or Town: Colfax

Physical Address: Steptoe Butte State Park, Colfax, WA 99111

GPS Coordinates: 47.0329° N, 117.2969° W

Did You Know? There was no water available in Steptoe State Park when the Chashup Hotel existed, so water had to be hauled up the butte each day by teams of horses so that hotel guests could have access to water.

Gifford Pinchot National Forest

Gifford Pinchot National Forest is a place the offers a bit of everything. At the Mount St. Helens National Volcanic Monument, there are 200 hiking trails.

Some are paved and perfect for a beginner, while others are more difficult hikes that will appeal to veteran hiking enthusiasts and backpackers. In the forest's 180,000 acres of wilderness, you can enjoy horseback riding, climbing, fishing, and hunting.

The Cowlitz Valley offers spectacular views of Mount St. Helens to the west, Mount Rainier to the north, and Mount Adams to the east. In the Mount Adams area, you'll find old-growth forests, wetland areas, glistening lakes, glaciers, and scenic meadows.

The Mount St. Helens area features spectacular crater views. The area also has opportunities to picnic, hike, and mountain bike at Smith Creek and venture into the Mount Margaret Backcountry.

Best Time to Visit: Late spring through early fall

Closest City or Town: Cougar

Physical Address: 1501 E. Evergreen Blvd. Vancouver, WA 98661

GPS Coordinates: 46.0626° N, 122.0292° W

Did You Know? The Gifford Pinchot National Forest covers 1,368,300 acres, which is bigger than the state of Delaware.

Sun Lakes-Dry Falls State Park

The Dry Falls surrounding Sun Lakes-Dry Falls State Park is one of the most extraordinary and visually striking geological wonders in the United States. The former waterfall was created by ice-age floods over 13,000 years ago and stood four times larger than Niagara Falls.

Now, the stark cliff is 400 feet tall and 3.5 miles wide. It overlooks a desert oasis full of reflective lakes and deep gorges. The historic Vista House Overlook offers panoramic views of Dry Falls.

The park is also a wonderful spot for outdoor recreation. Park Lake is great for boating and swimming, and Deep Lake is a perfect location for deep paddling and kayaking. Anglers love to visit Dry Falls Lake in search of trout. Plentiful hiking trails wind through the hills and cliffs with incredible views along the way.

Best Time to Visit: April through September

Closest City or Town: Coulee City

Physical Address: 34875 Park Lake Rd NE, Coulee City, WA 99115

GPS Coordinates: 47.6065° N, 119.3647° W

Did You Know? The flow of the floodwater that created Dry Falls is estimated to be ten times more powerful than the combined flow of every river on Earth.

Glacier Peak Wilderness

The Glacier Peak Wilderness takes up 566,057 acres of land and features 10,541-foot-tall Glacier Peak, which is the most remote major volcanic peak in the Cascade Range and the fourth-largest peak in the state. Wildlife in this area includes bears, cougars, lynx, wolverines, gray wolves, deer, elk, mountain goats, and martens. It's also a great spot for fishing cutthroat trout.

There are nearly 100 hiking trails ranging from easy to very advanced. The 8.3-mile Green Mountain Trail near Darrington, Washington features lovely wildflowers. For those less inclined toward hiking, there's horseback riding, bouldering, climbing, and navigating the glaciers.

The Ptarmigan Traverse is known as the most beautiful mountaineering route in the country. With its snowfields, high peaks, crystal-clear alpine lakes, and expansive views, it's not hard to see why.

Best Time to Visit: July to September

Closest City or Town: Darrington

Physical Address: NF-49, Darrington, WA 98241

GPS Coordinates: 48.1301° N, 121.2882° W

Did You Know? Glacier Peak is known for being the most explosive of the five volcanoes in Washington. Its last eruption was in 1700.

Blue Mountains

The Blue Mountains are often thought to be one of the best-kept hiking secrets in the state. Here, rushing rivers form deep caverns through the peaks. There are hundreds of trails through these picturesque mountains.

The best part is that even the most popular trails are less heavily trafficked than those in the Cascades, so you can avoid the crowds and enjoy the tranquility of nature around you with the big sky above.

The Bluewood Ski Area is a fantastic spot for tree skiing and powder. The area has a large Rocky Mountain elk population, so you may be lucky enough to spot one. Elk hunting is also popular, though it is strictly regulated by the Washington Fish and Wildlife Department.

Best Time to Visit: Early December to early April for skiing

Required Items: For information on Sno-Park permits, visit the Washington State Parks website. In case of rain, don't forget a waterproof jacket.

Closest City or Town: Dayton

Physical Address: Bluewood Rd, Dayton, WA 99328

GPS Coordinates: 46.1182° N, 117.7147° W

Did You Know? The range got its name from the beautiful blue color the mountains appear to have from a distance.

Lewis and Clark Trail State Park

Full of forests of maple, cottonwood, alder, and long-needled ponderosa trees, Lewis and Clark State Park is an oasis of lush greenness in the middle of the arid landscape of Southeastern Washington.

In 1806, the Lewis and Clark Corps of Discovery camped out in this area as they made their way home after their journey to the Pacific Coast.

This is a great spot for hiking and camping. With 1,333 feet of freshwater shoreline, Touchet River is also a popular location for wading, tubing, swimming, and fishing for rainbow trout.

Birdwatchers can delight in the orange-crowned warblers, red-tailed hawks, and common mergansers that inhabit the area. After a day of fun in the sun, you can visit the local winery half a mile east of the park for a nice glass of wine.

Best Time to Visit: April through October

Closest City or Town: Dayton

Physical Address: 36149 US-12, Dayton, WA 99328

GPS Coordinates: 46.2884° N, 118.0725° W

Did You Know? Woolly mammoth fossils—Washington state's official fossil—have been discovered in this area.

Olympic National Forest

The Olympic National Forest stretches out over 600,000 acres and almost surrounds the Olympic Mountain Range and Olympic National Park. The landscape of the forest varies quite a bit, from lush rainforests to tall mountain peaks to the saltwater fjord of Hood Canal.

In this forest, you'll find rushing rivers, abundant wildflowers, and large lowland lakes. From the mountaintops, you can see incredible views of Puget Sound.

The area is ideal for hiking, camping, biking, horseback riding, fishing, and picnicking. There are over 250 miles of hiking trails in Olympic National Forest, including eight nature trails with informational signs regarding the forest's history and unique features.

Best Time to Visit: The forest is open year round, but the rainforests can get a lot of rain in the winter, so the best time to visit them is spring through fall.

Closest City or Town: Eldon

Physical Address: Olympic National Forest, Washington 98363

GPS Coordinates: 47.5999° N, 123.1508° W

Did You Know? Nearly one-third of the Olympic National Forest is old growth, meaning the trees have grown without help from humans for hundreds of years.

Hoh Rainforest

Located in the Pacific Northwest, the Hoh Rainforest boasts three trails that take visitors through the area. The Hall of Mosses Trail passes through old-growth forest and features a maple tree grove covered with club moss.

The Spruce Trail winds through both old- and new-growth forest and alongside the Taft Creek and Hoh River. The Hoh River Trail is the main hiking path.

It's 18.5 miles long if you take it all the way to Blue Glacier, where you can view Mt. Olympus. Be prepared for rain since the Hoh Rainforest receives an average of 140 inches of precipitation each year.

Best Time to Visit: The best time to visit the Hoh Rainforest is during the summer after the spring rains have intensified the vegetation in the rainforest.

Pass/Permit/Fees: There is a fee of $11.50 per day to enter the Olympic National Park, where the Hoh Rainforest is located.

Closest City or Town: Forks

Physical Address: Hoh Rain Forest Visitor Center, 18113 Upper Hoh Rd, Forks, WA 98331

GPS Coordinates: 47.86148° N, 123.93475° W

Did You Know? The word *hoh* is a Native American word possibly derived from *ohalet* from the Quileute Tribe, which means "fast-moving water" or "snow water."

La Push Beach

La Push Beach is a series of three beaches: First Beach, Second Beach, and Third Beach. The northernmost beach, First Beach, has recreational activities to enjoy all year long. In fall and winter, you can storm watch. There's hiking in the summer, and you can fish and surf in the spring. It's also the only beach of the three that you can access with a vehicle, while the other two each require a bit of a hike.

Second Beach is the longest, flattest beach of the three. Here, you'll have a great view of sea stacks and surrounding islands. The Quillayute Needles National Wildlife Refuge protects various species of seabirds in the area, making it ideal for birdwatching. There's a 1.5-mile hike from the road to reach Third Beach, the most southern and secluded beach.

On the hike through the coastal forest, you'll find terrific views of Strawberry Bay. The beach features sea stacks and driftwood. In the cove at Taylor Point, there is also a picturesque waterfall and tidepools to explore.

Best Time to Visit: Summer

Closest City or Town: Forks

Physical Address: Ocean Front Dr, La Push, WA 98350

GPS Coordinates: 47.8906° N, 124.5992° W

Did You Know? The best time for spotting eagles is around 6 p.m. when they dive into the ocean to catch their dinner.

Rialto Beach

At Rialto Beach's rocky shores, you'll find crashing waves, huge drift logs, and magnificent views of offshore islands. A hike here will have you walking over rock, sand, and driftwood.

This is a fantastic location for wildlife viewing—there are eagles and seabirds in the sky and otters, sea lions, and whales offshore. There are also picnic tables near the parking lot where you can grab a snack or some lunch.

At a rocky arch called Hole-in-the-Wall, you can explore the tidepools and take in the marvelous views. Know that to get to Hole-in-the-Wall, you may need to get your feet wet crossing a creek. Mora Campground is just 3 miles from the beach and has 94 sites. The Mora area is surrounded by lush trees.

Best Time to Visit: April through October

Closest City or Town: Forks

Physical Address: Mora Rd, Forks, WA 98331

GPS Coordinates: 47.9173° N, 124.6394° W

Did You Know? Famed musician Claude Alexander Conlin named the beach after the Rialto theater chain.

Cattle Point Lighthouse

Cattle Point is the southernmost tip of San Juan Island. It got its name from when cattle first appeared at the point in 1853 after Hudson's Bay Company established a ranch there. The lighthouse overlooks the Strait of Juan de Fuca, where the Haro Straits meet the San Juan Channel and is a part of the San Juan Islands National Monument.

The hike to the lighthouse is short but sweet. Hiking around the windswept area, you'll see grassy dunes and plenty of birds. You may even spy a few golden eagles soaring through the wind in the sky above.

 Since the lighthouse is on a point, you will get phenomenal views from a few different angles. It's a great place to watch the sun rise or set. Next, the trail takes you down the water, where you can admire the glacier-carved, rocky beach.

Best Time to Visit: Late spring into autumn

Closest City or Town: Friday Harbor

Physical Address: Cattle Point Rd, Friday Harbor, WA 98250

GPS Coordinates: 48.4506° N, 122.9633° W

Did You Know? While a navigational lantern has remained at Cattle Point since 1888, the lighthouse wasn't built until 1935.

Lime Kiln Point State Park

Thanks to this small park's ample population of gray whales, orcas, and porpoises, Lime Kiln Point State Park is also known as Whale Watch Park. Many believe Lime Kiln Point, at the west end of San Juan Island, is one of the greatest whale-watching spots in the entire world. You can watch the whales from a sea cliff or perhaps from the historic Lime Kiln Lighthouse. Whale-watching boats and guided kayak trips are also available.

If whale watching isn't your thing, there's still lots of fun to experience here. Diving, hiking, and birdwatching are great activities to pursue during your visit. There are 12 picnic sites scattered along the shoreline and near the lighthouse as well.

Best Time to Visit: May through September for whale watching

Closest City or Town: Friday Harbor

Physical Address: 1567 West Side Rd, Friday Harbor, WA 98250

GPS Coordinates: 48.5160° N, 123.1510° W

Did You Know? The park is named for the lime kilns used in the area as part of a nineteenth-century lime-producing operation.

San Juan Islands

San Juan Islands is the name for 172 named islands located between Washington State and Vancouver Island, Canada. Three islands are serviced by ferries: Lopez Island, Orcas Island, and San Juan Island.

Numerous beaches, resorts, hotels, forests, and historic sites populate the islands, which offer visitors the opportunity for a quick day trip or a longer vacation stay. If you don't want to take a ferry to the islands, you can get there by flight (a wheeled passenger plane or seaplane) or by a private boat. In fact, getting to the San Juan Islands is half the fun!

Best Time to Visit: The best time to visit the San Juan Islands is during the summer when the temperatures hover in the 70s.

Pass/Permit/Fees: The fare to visit the San Juan Islands by ferry depends on your departure date, departing terminal, and arrival terminal.

Closest City or Town: Friday Harbor

Physical Address: 4668 Cattle Point Rd, Friday Harbor, WA 98250

GPS Coordinates: 48.53281° N, 123.01061° W

Did You Know? The San Juan Islands became part of Washington and the U.S. in 1872 when Kaiser Wilhelm I of Germany established the boundary line between the U.S. and Canada at the Haro Strait.

Mount Shuksan

Covered by a glacier, Mount Shuksan is less than 12 miles south of the U.S.–Canadian border. The mountain's highest point is a three-sided peak called the Summit Pyramid. Mt. Baker Ski Area is located on the mountain, so the Mount Baker Highway is open year round, but the road to Artist Point is only open in late summer to allow visitors an opportunity to get closer to the peak.

Picture Lake, one of the most photographed spots in the state, is located just off the highway and provides a crystal-clear reflection of the mountain, which is why it's so popular. Other features found on the mountain include Sulphide Creek Falls and four other tall waterfalls.

Best Time to Visit: The best time to visit Mount Shuksan for skiing is in the winter, but for all other activities, summer is the prime season.

Pass/Permit/Fees: There is no fee to visit Mount Shuksan.

Closest City or Town: Glacier

Physical Address: Mt Baker Hwy, Deming, WA 98244

GPS Coordinates: 48.83310° N, 121.60360° W

Did You Know? Mount Shuksan's name is from the Lummi word *seqsen*, which is believed to mean "high peak."

Mt. Baker-Snoqualmie National Forest

The Mt. Baker-Snoqualmie National Forest is one of the most popular forests to visit in the U.S. It's situated on the west side of the Cascades between the Canadian border and Mount Rainier National Park. The forest is full of ancient trees, glacier-covered peaks, and beautiful mountain meadows.

Mountains are 5,000 to 6,000 feet tall on the south side of the forest, while in the north, they rise 7,000 to 8,000 feet. The forest is also home to Mt. Baker, a towering volcano.

Whether you're a veteran of the outdoors or a new hiker, you will find a great adventure here. The forest offers a little bit of everything—bird watching, river rafting, fishing, skiing, snowshoeing, and more.

Best Time to Visit: With lovely hikes in the spring, summer, and fall, and skiing and snowshoeing in the winter, this is a wonderful destination all year long.

Closest City or Town: Glacier

Physical Address: WA-542, Deming, WA 98244

GPS Coordinates: 48.8548° N, 121.6858° W

Did You Know? The Mt. Baker-Snoqualmie National Forest contains more glaciers and snowfields than any of the other national forests in the lower 48 states.

Wallace Falls State Park

There's no shortage of forests, lakes, and waterfalls in Washington, but no place manages to showcase these iconic features of the landscape quite like Wallace Falls State Park.

With the park's many glorious trails, hikers will swear they've died and gone to heaven. You can hike or snowshoe up the Wallace River to mighty Wallace Falls. Those searching for a longer hike can follow the Greg Ball Trail to the Wallace and Jay lakes.

Other activities to enjoy in the park include rock climbing and swimming. People have spotted several cougars near Wallace Falls, and peregrine falcons inhabit the rock cliffs of the Index Town Wall. The park is great for camping, and there are also cabins available to reserve that accommodate up to five guests each.

Best Time to Visit: April until November

Closest City or Town: Gold Bar

Physical Address: 14503 Wallace Lake Road, Gold Bar, WA 98251

GPS Coordinates: 47.8992° N, 121.6718° W

Did You Know? The name *Wallace* is derived from the surname of Joe and Sarah Kwayaylsh, the members of the Skykomish tribe who became the first homesteaders in the area.

Steamboat Rock State Park

teamboat Rock State Park stretches across 3,522 acres. The land was carved at least 13,000 years ago by ice-age floods into a breathtaking canyon that features several lakes. The hike to the top of Steamboat Rock offers stunning views of Grand Coulee and the majestic mountains of the Okanogan-Wenatchee National Forest with the blue lake below. At an 800-foot elevation and with a surface area of 600 acres, Steamboat Rock offers many wonders to behold for avid hikers.

This park is also a great place for water sports, with seven watercraft launches and 320 feet of docks on Banks Lake. Northrup Canyon offers plenty of fun for mountain biking and horseback riding enthusiasts. This place is a well-loved camping park with three campground areas that are protected from strong winds by towering poplar trees. There are three cabins available for rent in the Bay Loop as well that can accommodate up to five guests.

Best Time to Visit: Year round

Closest City or Town: Grand Coulee

Physical Address: 51052 WA-155, Electric City, WA 99123

GPS Coordinates: 47.8635° N, 119.1227° W

Did You Know? There is a Native American legend that Steamboat Rock was created when Eagle refused to let Coyote marry his daughter.

Point No Point

This unusually named location at the tip of the Kitsap Peninsula is an outcropping of land that is also home to a lighthouse and one of the largest populations of birds in the state. Numerous water-related bird species flock to Point No Point, including loons, terns, gulls, jaegers, ducks, cormorants, scoters, grebes, and more.

The outcropping was named Point No Point because the tip of the peninsula appears significantly more prominent from a distance than up close.

Best Time to Visit: The best time to visit Point No Point is during the summer when the weather is warmer.

Pass/Permit/Fees: There is no fee to visit Point No Point.

Closest City or Town: Hansville

Physical Address: 9009 NE Point No Point Rd, Hansville, WA 98340

GPS Coordinates: 47.9146° N, 122.5270° W

Did You Know? Point No Point got its name from Charles Wilkes when he was exploring Puget Sound as a part of the United States Exploring Expedition of 1841.

Lake Cushman

Due to Lake Cushman's crystal-clear waters and lush forested shoreline, this reservoir is an extremely popular destination for swimming, boating, fishing, and picnicking. It receives such high amounts of weather-dependent visitation that the roads reaching the reservoir can be packed on sunny weekends, with the only turnaround available at the Staircase entrance of Olympic National Park. As such, you'll want to leave early if you intend to spend a day at Lake Cushman, or you should choose a time of year that sees fewer crowds. Fishing is open year round, and the lake is stocked with rainbow trout. You may also pull kokanee or cutthroat from the water as well. Swimming is available at the Bear Gulch Day Use Area and Big Creek Campground.

Best Time to Visit: If you enjoy crowds, the best time to visit is in the summer. Otherwise, choose the spring or fall.

Pass/Permit/Fees: There is a $15-per-vehicle fee to visit Lake Cushman.

Closest City or Town: Hoodsport

Physical Address: 7211 N Lake Chushman Rd, Hoodsport, WA 98548

GPS Coordinates: 47.4935° N, 123.2538° W

Did You Know? Lake Cushman takes its name from Orrington Cushman, who was an interpreter for Governor Isaac Stevens during the negotiations with Puget Sound Native Americans that resulted in the Treaty of Point Elliott in 1854.

Cape Disappointment

Located on the southwestern corner of Washington State, Cape Disappointment is a headland where the Pacific Ocean meets the Columbia River. Cape Disappointment State Park and the historic Cape Disappointment Lighthouse are both located here. The Cape Disappointment Lighthouse was built in 1856 and is the oldest lighthouse in the Pacific Northwest that is still in operation. There is also the operational North Head Lighthouse, which is an easier hike.

The views on the hiking trails of 2,023-acre Cape Disappointment State Park are awe-inspiring—they will take you around blue lakes, old-growth forests, rugged beaches, and saltwater marshes. Baker Bay is a popular location for boating, while Benson Beach is great for fishing salmon and crab, as well as digging for clams. The park has 137 campsites, and yurts and cabins are also available for rent.

Best Time to Visit: June through September

Closest City or Town: Ilwaco

Physical Address: 244 Robert Gray Dr, Ilwaco, WA 98624

GPS Coordinates: 46.2996° N, 124.0654° W

Did You Know? Like Mount Olympus, Cape Disappointment was named by British fur trader John Meares in 1788. The sea captain approached the cape but could not find the river's entrance, much to his "disappointment."

Lake Sammamish State Park

Lake Sammamish State Park takes up 531 acres and has 6,858 feet of waterfront on Lake Sammamish. With two lakefront beaches (Tibbetts Beach and Sunset Beach), the park is a fantastic spot for a beach day. It's a popular place for boating, waterskiing, and other watersports. The park includes a boat launch where visitors can park their vehicles and boat trailers.

This park is yet another wonderful hiking location with its many trails through wetlands and deciduous forests. Bald eagles and blue herons nest in the park, so keep an eye out! For more wildlife-viewing opportunities, there's also a great blue heron rookery and a salmon-bearing creek. There is a state-of-the-art playground for children and picnic areas for the whole family.

Best Time to Visit: Summer is ideal for swimming and kayaking.

Closest City or Town: Issaquah

Physical Address: 2000 NW Sammamish Rd, Issaquah, WA 98027

GPS Coordinates: 47.5600° N, 122.0555° W

Did You Know? Before Washington State Parks bought the land in 1950, this area was farmed for 70 years. And before *that*, the land was inhabited by Native Americans for thousands of years.

La Conner

Consistently voted as the most perfect weekend getaway destination in Washington State, La Conner is a charming town located on the Salish Sea between Seattle and Vancouver. Home to the Skagit Valley Tulip Festival, La Conner receives hundreds of thousands of visitors each year with most of them showing up in April to see the tulips in bloom. There is another flower festival in La Conner, as the Daffodil Festival precedes the tulip celebration by a month. This is an excellent way to avoid the crowds at the Tulip Festival but still get to see acres of cheery flowers in the Skagit Valley. In addition to the actual festivals, La Conner hosts more than 20 events in April alone and boasts three nationally recognized museums.

Best Time to Visit: The best time to visit La Conner is during March or April when either the daffodil or tulip festival is underway.

Pass/Permit/Fees: There is no fee to visit La Conner.

Closest City or Town: La Conner

Physical Address: Tulip Fields, 14520-14998 Young Rd, Mt Vernon, WA 98273

GPS Coordinates: 48.3951° N, 122.4919° W

Did You Know? La Conner got its name from J.S. Conner, who purchased the trading post at the Swinomish channel in 1869 and named the town in honor of his wife, Louisa Ann Conner.

Skagit Valley Bulb Fields

During the annual Skagit Valley Tulip Festival, Tulip Town and RoozenGaarde bulb fields invite visitors to view their incredible tulip fields, tulip gardens, indoor tulip displays, and much more. Tulip Town also offers a variety of hands-on experiences such as picking your own bouquet, visiting the barn, and photographing the fields. At RoozenGaarde, visitors can access the 25-acre tulip field and the 20-acre daffodil field for photographs and sightseeing. The Tulip Festival, when the tulips are in bloom, runs from April 1 to April 30 each year, but on occasion, the tulips may not bloom until the second week of April. In most years, they bloom the last week of March.

Best Time to Visit: The best time to visit the Skagit Valley Bulb Fields is during April. Mid-to-late April is best to ensure the tulips have bloomed.

Pass/Permit/Fees: The tulip fields can be viewed for free from your vehicle, but the Tulip Town and RoozenGaarde experiences are $15 per person for visitors. Tulip Town has a discounted price of $5 for children between the ages of 6 and 11.

Closest City or Town: La Conner

Physical Address: Tulip Town, 15002 Bradshaw Rd, Mt Vernon, WA 98273

GPS Coordinates: 48.42873° N, 122.42383° W

Did You Know? In the two main tulip fields of Tulip Town and RoozenGaarde, more than 1 million tulip bulbs bloom each year.

Alpine Lakes Wilderness

The Alpine Lakes Wilderness is one of the most popular locations for outdoor recreation activities in the state. It encompasses roughly 394,000 acres of the Central Cascades region. It has over 600 miles of hiking trails and is accessible by 47 different trailheads.

The wilderness features more than 700 lakes and mountain ponds. Several peaks and slopes of the surrounding Cascades are permanently covered in snow.

This diverse landscape also includes expansive meadows and dry forestland. In the Enchantment Lakes area, you'll find the Cashmere Crags, which are known for being one of the best rock-climbing sites in the western U.S.

Best Time to Visit: July through October

Closest City or Town: Leavenworth

Physical Address: Eightmile Trailhead, NF-7601, Leavenworth, WA 98826

GPS Coordinates: 47.6091° N, 120.9450° W

Did You Know? When President Ford signed the law protecting the Alpine Lakes Wilderness Area in 1976, he allegedly said, "Anywhere so beautiful should be preserved."

Colchuck Lake

This freshwater reservoir can only be accessed by a 4-mile trail that begins at U.S. Forest Service Road 7601 and ends at Colchuck Lake Trailhead. The lake is about 88 acres in size and stores about 1,570 acre-feet of water. It is contained by a dam that was built in the 1930s to control overflow and currently serves as water storage for irrigation.

The main attraction of Colchuck Lake for visitors is the Colchuck Lake Trail, which provides stunning views of the water and the twin spires of Colchuck and Dragontail peaks. The trail can be challenging in areas, particularly on the final ascent to the lake, which is steep and rugged. Hikers can also access Stuart Lake from this trail.

Best Time to Visit: The best time to visit Colchuck Lake is during the summer and early fall.

Pass/Permit/Fees: A valid recreation pass or a fee of $5 per vehicle, per day is required to visit Colchuck Lake.

Closest City or Town: Leavenworth

Physical Address: Colchuck Lake Trailhead, NF-7601, Leavenworth, WA 98826

GPS Coordinates: 47.4923° N, 120.8331° W

Did You Know? Colchuck Lake got its name from the Chinook words *kol* and *cak*, which mean "cold waters."

Front Street Park

As Leavenworth, Washington's main recreation center, Front Street Park is ideally situated in the business area of town. Locals and visitors can easily access entertainment, festivals, shopping, and other events from the park, which is beautifully landscaped with alpine gardens, a gazebo, a maypole, and towering shade trees. A main feature of the park is its *Art in the Park* exhibit, which showcases work from various artists along the park's plaza. The gazebo is primarily used as an outdoor performing arts stage, and there is entertainment available almost daily. Some of the more popular events that occur in the park include Christkindlmarkt, the Christmas Lighting Festival, Icefest, Leavenworth Spring Bird Festival, Kinderfest, Maifest, and Oktoberfest, among others.

Best Time to Visit: There is something to see in this park no matter when you visit, but for the best weather, visit in the summer.

Pass/Permit/Fees: There is no fee to visit Front Street Park.

Closest City or Town: Leavenworth

Physical Address: 820 Front St, Leavenworth, WA 98826

GPS Coordinates: 47.5963° N, 120.6619° W

Did You Know? The sledding hill in Front Street Park is one of the most popular winter activities in Leavenworth, but be sure to bring your own sled!

Icicle Gorge

Icicle Gorge is a small but scenic canyon surrounding Icicle Creek, a tributary of the Wenatchee River that flows near Leavenworth. The gorge is located in the Okanogan-Wenatchee National Forest and offers various hiking opportunities throughout the area.

The most popular access point to the gorge is through the Icicle Gorge Trailhead, which is situated approximately 30 minutes west of Leavenworth.

Once you get into the gorge, the trails branch off from the main path to both sides of the creek and up into the forest above it. Regardless of which trail you take, you're sure to see spectacular views, waterfalls, and colorful foliage.

Best Time to Visit: The best time to visit Icicle Gorge is during the spring, summer, or early fall.

Pass/Permit/Fees: There is a $5 per-vehicle fee to day hike within the Okanogan-Wenatchee National Forest.

Closest City or Town: Leavenworth

Physical Address: Okanogan-Wenatchee National Forest, Wenatchee, WA 98807

GPS Coordinates: 47.6090° N, 120.8944° W

Did You Know? The wildflowers in Icicle Gorge that are in bloom during the spring include wild roses, stone crop, dogwoods, lupine, columbine, goatsbeard, salmonberry, hawksbeard, Indian paintbrush, and many more.

Icicle Ridge Trail

This picturesque trail near Leavenworth is a 5.5-mile trail for walking, mountain biking, and horseback riding that is rated as moderate. The well-maintained path keeps the trail from being too challenging, especially during the winter months, when the area can get snow.

The views at the end of the trail offer a 360-degree look at the surrounding mountainous landscape. It is one of the few trails in the area that can be snow free by April, which means hikers can get an early glimpse of spring with lush forests of maples, Ponderosa pines, and colorful wildflowers.

Best Time to Visit: The best time to visit Icicle Ridge Trail is during the spring to see the wildflowers in bloom and a seasonal waterfall, but it's an excellent hike in summer and fall as well.

Pass/Permit/Fees: There is no fee to visit Icicle Ridge Trail.

Closest City or Town: Leavenworth

Physical Address: Okanogan-Wenatchee National Forest, Wenatchee, WA 98807

GPS Coordinates: 47.5695° N, 120.6813° W

Did You Know? Poison ivy is abundant along the Icicle Ridge Trail, so be sure to watch out for the leaves and avoid contact with them.

Lake Stuart

Located in the famous Enchantments, Lake Stuart offers a peaceful locale in an otherwise heavily visited area. While most hikers take the Lake Stuart trailhead to travel to the core zone by way of Colchuck Lake, you can choose the less-traveled right-hand trail that takes you to Lake Stuart itself, a large, shallow lake that is located at the base of Mount Stuart.

This 2.2-mile path will take you through marshland that's covered with trillium far into the summer. You'll also cross Mountaineer Creek using a log bridge that was installed in 2014 as a replacement to the aging original. When you get to a junction that is 2 miles from the trailhead, be sure to bear right or you'll end up at Colchuck Lake instead of Lake Stuart.

Best Time to Visit: The best time to visit Lake Stuart is during the summer, as it is often too cold to visit during the other seasons.

Pass/Permit/Fees: There is a $5-per-vehicle fee to visit the Enchantments.

Closest City or Town: Leavenworth

Physical Address: Forest Service Road 7601, Leavenworth, WA 98826

GPS Coordinates:47.4972° N, 120.8770° W

Did You Know? Camping is available in the forest near Lake Stuart as long as you obtain an overnight camping permit.

Leavenworth

This small mountain town is designed to resemble an old-world Bavarian village. It is reminiscent of a German town nestled in a valley and surrounded by snow-topped mountains. If you're looking to get a taste of Germany without leaving the U.S., Leavenworth likely has everything you want.

There are numerous specialty shops, unique restaurants, relaxing spas, and plenty of lodging options. Wine tasting, fruit orchards, breweries, distilleries, museums, parks, bicycle tours, art and theater, hiking, mountain biking, whitewater rafting, and skiing are all activities that attract visitors to this quaint town.

Best Time to Visit: Orchards are in bloom in the summer, the leaves are spectacular in the fall, and the Village of Lights Christmastown is a must-see attraction in winter.

Pass/Permit/Fees: There is no fee to visit Leavenworth, but some activities will charge separate fees.

Closest City or Town: Leavenworth

Physical Address: 940 US-2 Suite B, Leavenworth, WA 98826

GPS Coordinates: 47.5995° N, 120.6591° W

Did You Know? Leavenworth was incorporated in 1906 as a small timber community that eventually became a regional office for the Great Northern Railroad until it relocated in 1925.

Perfection Lake

Perfection Lake is part of what is known as the Enchantments, a mountainous area of Washington State that features crystal-blue lakes formed by glaciers that are connected by a creek flowing between them. Perfection Lake is aptly named, as its surface is perfectly clear. It's shallow, but the smooth, glassy water is ideal for nature photographs.

The trek to Perfection Lake is fairly rigorous and will require at least a day trip to hike there and back. The Enchantments Trail to reach various lakes in the area is 20.5 miles long one way.

Best Time to Visit: The best time to visit Perfection Lake is during the fall, as the foliage and views are more dramatic.

Pass/Permit/Fees: There is a fee of $5 per vehicle per day to enter the forest where the lake is located.

Closest City or Town: Leavenworth

Physical Address: NF-7601, Leavenworth, WA 98826

GPS Coordinates: 47.48006° N, 120.79738° W

Did You Know? On the way to Perfection Lake, you'll pass Colchuck Lake, Tranquil Lake, Isolation Lake, Crystal Lake, and Inspiration Lake.

Long Beach

Unsurprisingly, Long Beach got its name from being a very long beach. There's an archway in the town of Long Beach that proclaims the beach to be "The World's Longest Beach," which it is not. But at roughly 28 miles long, Long Beach *is* the world's longest continuous beach on a peninsula. Here, you can sunbathe to your heart's content, enjoy picnics, and go horseback riding. The beach is also a great spot to watch for birds and whales or go fishing, oystering, and crabbing.

Long Beach is home to the annual Washington State International Kite Festival, where you can watch expert kite fliers fill the sky with vibrant colors. Another thing that makes Long Beach unique is that it's a beach you can drive on. There's nothing quite like driving across the sand with the waves crashing beside you. Just remember to keep to the right and obey the 25-mph speed limit.

Best Time to Visit: If you want to catch the Washington International Kite Festival, it takes place during the third week of August.

Closest City or Town: Long Beach

Physical Address: 3914 Pacific Way, Seaview, WA 98644

GPS Coordinates: 46.3306° N, 124.0635° W

Did You Know? More than 150 species of birds live on the peninsula, including the endangered snowy plover and the great horned owl.

Lopez Hill

Lopez Hill covers 400 acres, with the hill standing at 535 feet tall. The area is a dream come true for nature lovers and hiking enthusiasts. If you're looking for a challenge, a network of hiking trails weaves its way through thick-growth forests, canyons, moss-covered rock outcroppings, and prairie land.

In addition to hikers, the trails are open to mountain bikers and equestrians as well (though some trails are only open to horses on a seasonal basis). Lopez Hill is also a popular destination for hunters.

There's a wide range of island flora to behold, including lichens, fungi, wildflowers, and more. The summit affords glorious views of the Strait of Juan de Fuca and beyond. You could easily spend more than one day enjoying the natural wonders of Lopez Hill.

Best Time to Visit: Year round

Closest City or Town: Lopez Island

Physical Address: Lopez Sound Rd, Lopez Island, WA 98261

GPS Coordinates: 48.4816° N, 122.8698° W

Did You Know? The Lopez Hill trails are built and maintained entirely by volunteers. The Friends of Lopez Hill is an organization are dedicated to preserving Lopez Hill's natural beauty and recreational value.

Columbia River Gorge National Scenic Area

The Columbia River Gorge is a vast, 4,000-foot-deep canyon that forms the boundary of Washington to the north and Oregon to the south. Here, you can see the Columbia River flow right through the Cascade Mountain Range. The diverse landscape spans between dry grasslands and temperate rainforests. The forests are full of western hemlock, bigleaf maples, and Douglas fir.

The deep cut of the gorge is a popular location for kiteboarding and windsurfing thanks to the atmospheric pressure differentials east and west of the Cascades that generate 35-mph winds. This is a great area for biking, hiking, water sports, and salmon fishing. There's a wealth of amazing panoramic views to be seen along the Pacific Crest Trail. Cape Horn is strenuous but will reward you with sights of wildflowers, waterfalls, and several species of birds.

Best Time to Visit: Late April through June for wildflowers, July and August for ideal weather

Closest City or Town: Lyle

Physical Address: NF-18, Mt Hood, OR 97041

GPS Coordinates: 45.6993° N, 121.2935° W

Did You Know? Humans have inhabited the Columbia River Gorge for over 13,000 years.

Diablo Lake

This reservoir is located in the North Cascade Mountains and was created by the Diablo Dam. There are two other lakes flanking the sides of Lake Diablo, which are Ross Lake and Gorge Lake. Diablo Lake is a component of the Skagit River Hydroelectric Project and is home to Diablo Lake Trail, a 3.8-mile hike that follows the lake's northern shore.

The Skagit River Hydroelectric Project is a series of dams that generate hydroelectric power, which serves to provide electric power to Seattle and the surrounding communities. The lake is a popular fishing spot for rainbow trout, brook, bull trout, and coastal cutthroat, and it's also an excellent place for kayaking and canoeing.

Best Time to Visit: The best time to visit Diablo Lake is in the summer, particularly for fishermen and boaters.

Pass/Permit/Fees: There is no fee to visit Diablo Lake.

Closest City or Town: Marblemount

Physical Address: State Rte 20, Rockport, WA 98283

GPS Coordinates: 48.7114° N, 121.1144° W

Did You Know? Diablo Lake's turquoise color comes from the surrounding glaciers that have ground rocks into a fine power known as glacial flour. It stays suspended in the lake, providing color to the water.

Horseshoe Basin

Located in the upper Stehekin River Valley, Horseshoe Basin is a particularly awe-inspiring sight to see. It lies between the Park Creek Pass and the Stehekin River Road.

Orange granite spires ring the lip of the basin as glistening waterfalls crash down into the valley. There are wildflowers as far as the eye can see. If you're lucky, you might catch sight of a black bear—just don't get too close!

Hiking in and out of Horseshoe Basin is not for the faint of heart. The trek is between 12 and 17 miles round trip depending on which route you take, and the trip involves a great deal of climbing.

Instead of trying to do everything all in one day, you could elect to camp overnight at Pelton Basin.

Best Time to Visit: July through September

Closest City or Town: Marblemount

Physical Address: Pelton Basin Campground, Marblemount, WA 98267

GPS Coordinates: 48.4857° N, 121.0215° W

Did You Know? Horseshoe Basin is home to the Black Warrior Mine, which operated until the mid-1950s and is listed on the National Register of Historic Places.

Methow Valley

The Methow Valley is the name of a collection of towns, mountains, rivers, lakes, and trails in the foothills of the North Cascades mountain range. From the popular fishing confluence of the Methow and Columbia rivers in Pateros to the Methow Valley Interpretive Center, the Twisp River Recreation Area to the Wild West town of Winthrop, you'll find plenty of activities and attractions to visit.

You'll probably have to stay a few nights to make sure you get a taste of all there is to see and do in Methow Valley. Fishing, river rafting, tubing, hunting, camping, rock climbing, shopping, and sightseeing are all reasons to visit the towns of Pateros, Winthrop, and Mazama. Consider taking the Cascade Loop to see it all!

Best Time to Visit: The best time to visit the Methow Valley is during the summer, but there are plenty of winter activities available as well.

Pass/Permit/Fees: There is no fee to visit the Methow Valley, but individual activities will have various costs.

Closest City or Town: Mazama

Physical Address: Methow Recreation Free Area, 431 Methow Valley Hwy, Twisp, WA 98856

GPS Coordinates: 48.6888° N, 120.4624° W

Did You Know? The Methow Valley is named for the Methow tribe that lived in the area before the early 1900s.

Padilla Bay

Padilla Bay is located between the San Juan Islands and the mainland. It's an estuary of the Skagit River. Hiking along the bay is perfect for beginners. On your hike, you'll see a piece of history—an old barn that once belonged to a "stump farm," which is the name for cheap land purchased after the logging area was converted to farming in the early 1900s.

Great blue herons like to hunt around the barn, so keep an eye out for them. You also might catch sight of northern harriers along the shoreline and roses growing wild along the ditch. Birdsong will accompany you on your journey.

At low tide, the water will recede from the bay, and you can see the mudflats. At a small promontory, there's a chance to take a rest on a bench to admire the views of Lummi Island and Mount Baker. In the winter, you might spy a snowy owl.

Best Time to Visit: Year round

Closest City or Town: Mount Vernon

Physical Address: Padilla Bay Trailhead, Shore Trail, Mt Vernon, WA 98273

GPS Coordinates: 48.4571° N, 122.4661° W

Did You Know? Padilla means "bread pan" in Spanish.

Cleman Mountain

The impressively large Cleman Mountain can be seen from pretty much anywhere in the Yakima or Naches valleys. As the tallest thing in the area, the mountain's summit affords incredible panoramic views of Mount Adams, the William O. Douglas Area, and the Goat Rocks.

In the winter, goats, elk, and other animals are easily found wandering the area. Hiking here, you'll see lovely views over the orchards of Naches Heights and the Naches Valley and down into Waterworks and Meystre canyons.

The climb can range from fairly easy to very difficult depending on the weather and how far you plan to go. A jaunt through the canyon is simple, but reaching the summit requires a great deal of stamina and physical fitness.

Best Time to Visit: May for wildflowers, September and October for color and wildlife

Closest City or Town: Naches

Physical Address: N Wenas Rd, Washington, 98937

GPS Coordinates: 46.7487° N, 120.7970° W

Did You Know? The Cleman Mountain Lookout was originally developed in 1946 with a log cabin.

Cape Flattery

Cape Flattery has the distinction of being the most northwesterly point in the lower 48 states. It is also the Olympic Coast National Marine Sanctuary's northern boundary. From the tip of the scenic Cape Flattery Trail, you can see a lovely view of Tatoosh Island.

You might spy some sea lions on Snake Rock, which lies east of Tatoosh Island. Gray whales are also often sighted off the cape. There are four different observation decks on the trail, which provide amazing views of birds, craggy rocks, and gorgeous Pacific waters.

Depending on the weather and cloud cover, the Pacific may appear to be a variety of different colors, including shades like light yellow and pink at sunset. You can enjoy a packed lunch or snack at one of the picnic tables at the end of the trail.

Best Time to Visit: Year round

Closest City or Town: Neah Bay

Physical Address: Cape Loop Rd, Neah Bay, WA 98357

GPS Coordinates: 48.3831° N, 124.7144° W

Did You Know? Named by British explorer James Cook in 1788, Cape Flattery is the oldest permanently named feature in the state.

Shi Shi Beach

Located in Olympic National Park on the Makah Indian Reservation, Shi Shi Beach is a sandy stretch along the Pacific Ocean that is popular for hiking and birdwatching. It is approximately 1.3 miles long and features eagles and seabirds gliding along the shore. The Shi Shi Beach Trail is a local favorite because it features both beach walking and rainforest hiking.

The entire trail is approximately 2.5 miles and ends at the Point of Arches. This location is excellent for a day trip, but it's also a well-known spot for backpacking and spending the night on the beach. Shi Shi Beach was incorporated into the Olympic National Park in 1976 and is currently being renovated for easier access.

Best Time to Visit: The best time to visit Shi Shi Beach is during the summer for the warmer temperatures.

Pass/Permit/Fees: A $10 recreation permit from the Makah Indian Reservation is required to visit Shi Shi Beach.

Closest City or Town: Neah Bay

Physical Address: Fish Hatchery Rd, Neah Bay, WA 98357

GPS Coordinates: 48.2618° N, 124.6834° W

Did You Know? Shi Shi Beach was awarded the title of "Best Nature Beach" by the Travel Channel.

Ross Lake National Recreation Area

As the most accessible portion of the North Cascades National Park Service Complex, Ross Lake National Recreation Area is a popular destination for hiking, camping, boating, fishing, and more. Within the recreation area, there are three reservoirs: Ross Lake, Gorge Lake, and Diablo Lake.

Whether you want to explore the area yourself, or you're looking for ranger-led programs or naturalist tours, you'll be awestruck at the vistas, wildlife, and plant life you see. There are at least 75 documented mammal species, 21 reptile species, 200 bird species, 28 fish species, and 500 types of land insects in the park. If you're lucky, you may even be able to catch a glimpse of the elusive gray wolf.

Best Time to Visit: The best time to visit Ross Lake National Recreation Area is between mid-June and late September.

Pass/Permit/Fees: There is no fee to visit Ross Lake National Recreation Area.

Closest City or Town: Newhalem

Physical Address: 810 WA-20, Rockport, WA 98283

GPS Coordinates: 48.7641° N, 121.0596° W

Did You Know? Desolation Peak Lookout, located in Ross Lake National Recreation Area, is the setting for Jack Kerouac's novel *Desolation Angels*.

Colville National Forest

Many people might think that Washington is entirely flat on the eastern side of the Cascades, but Colville National Forest proves that they are mistaken. This forest was formed by ice-age glaciers 10,000 years ago and spanned across 1.5 million acres.

It features the major valleys of the San Poil-Curlew, Pend Oreille, and Columbia rivers. Troughs of valleys separate the Kettle River, Selkirk, and Okanogan mountain ranges. The forest is full of glistening lakes, rivers, and streams.

With 486 miles of hiking trails, the forest is a wonderful hiking destination. The area is also great for horseback riding, mountain biking, and camping. The forest serves as a habitat for bald eagles, cougars, and grizzly bears. Colville is also home to the last remaining caribou herd in the country.

Best Time to Visit: Year round

Closest City or Town: Newport

Physical Address: Pioneer Park Campground, 1061, Le Clerc Rd S, Usk, WA 99180

GPS Coordinates: 48.1903° N, 117.0533° W

Did You Know? The Colville Forest Reserve was created by Theodore Roosevelt on March 1, 1907.

Riverside State Park

No matter what type of activities you enjoy, there are plenty of recreational opportunities for you at Riverside State Park. You can go mountain biking, hiking, rock climbing, horseback riding, and more.

There are 55 miles of hiking and mountain-biking trails with various paths to suit every possible level of experience. Hiking around the Bowl and Pitcher area, you'll get beautiful views of the impressive Spokane River, towering Ponderosa firs, and rocky outcroppings.

The park has 25 miles of equestrian trails, an obstacle course, and a horse-friendly campground. This is also a good area for winter and summer sports. The Bowl and Pitcher Campground features 16 standard campsites.

Best Time to Visit: Year round

Closest City or Town: Nine Mile Falls

Physical Address: 9711 W Charles Rd, Nine Mile Falls, WA 99026

GPS Coordinates: 47.7542° N, 117.5488° W

Did You Know? Riverside was historically a fur-trading hub for Native Americans.

Granite Mountain

There are a few different peaks called "Granite Mountain" in the state, but this tall one alongside I-90 has proven the most popular. Granite Mountain is another hike that is not going to be a walk in the park—you need to be in good shape for this one.

The hike itself is only 8.6 miles round trip, but you'll have to climb 3,800 feet to a lookout with an elevation of 5,629 feet. The views of the Central Cascades are well worth the effort. On this hike, you'll be able to see every volcano in the state except for Mount St. Helens.

The route features high alpine meadows, towering hemlocks, and a historic lookout tower at the summit. Huckleberry bushes line the trail and in late summer can provide a tasty snack. Keep an eye out for pikas on your way, which are common in the area.

Best Time to Visit: Summer for wildflowers and fall for color

Closest City or Town: North Bend

Physical Address: NF-9034 aWA 98045QQA KO, North Bend, WA 98045

GPS Coordinates: 47.3979° N, 121.4866° W

Did You Know? A 1916 mountaineer's journal describes a summer forest lookout station at the summit of Granite Mountain.

Kendall Katwalk

The name *Kendall Katwalk* may make you a little nervous. Perhaps you're picturing a narrow path on a cliff face, and that is definitely one aspect of it.

But here, you will also see an old-growth forest, exquisite wildflowers, and spectacular views of the Alpine Lakes Wilderness from both sides of the pass below Kendall Peak. In late August and early September, you might get the chance to pick some fresh blueberries growing along the trail.

Slopes that feature penstemon, lupine, columbine, paintbrush, and phlox are known as Kendall Gardens. Lingering snow can make this gorgeous and dangerous to traverse, though, so be sure to check trail conditions before you arrive.

Best Time to Visit: June until September

Closest City or Town: North Bend

Physical Address: Pacific Crest Trail, North Bend, WA 98045

GPS Coordinates: 47.4522° N, 121.3787° W

Did You Know? The Kendall Katwalk was created many years ago by using dynamite to blast a path from Kendall Ridge's sheer granite wall.

Olallie State Park

More than anything else, Olallie State Park is known for its awe-inspiring waterfalls. Hiking trails lead to the mighty Twin Falls, as well as the smaller Weeks Falls and many other waterfalls.

Ambitious mountain bikers can attempt the 20-mile Olallie Trail, which provides gorgeous views of the rushing river, lush forests, and unique rock formations of the Snoqualmie Valley.

There are also numerous cliffs for mountain climbing enthusiasts to enjoy. There is excellent fishing on the South Fork of the Snoqualmie River as well. And when you need a break, you can have some lunch at the South Fork Picnic Area.

Best Time to Visit: Year round. The river is seasonally open for fishing.

Closest City or Town: North Bend

Physical Address: 51350 SE Homestead Valley Rd, North Bend, WA 98045

GPS Coordinates: 47.4530° N, 121.7054° W

Did You Know? In 1977, the park's name was changed from Twin Falls State Park to Olallie, the Chinook Jargon word for *salmonberry*, due to the abundance of berries in the area.

Rattlesnake Lake

Rattlesnake Lake is a day-use recreational lake located in the Rattlesnake Mountain Scenic Area. During the summer, Rattlesnake Lake is a popular destination for fishing and birdwatching.

When the water level is low, many tree stumps become exposed and are used as nesting sites by various bird species. On-shore activities include picnicking and hiking the Rattlesnake Ledge Hiking Trail, which climbs 1,160 feet over 2 miles.

The hiking trail leads from the north shore of Rattlesnake Lake to the Rattlesnake Ledge scenic overlook that offers spectacular views of the lake and valley.

Best Time to Visit: The best time to visit Rattlesnake Lake is during the summer.

Pass/Permit/Fees: There is no fee to visit Rattlesnake Lake.

Closest City or Town: North Bend

Physical Address: 17905 Cedar Falls Rd SE, North Bend, WA 98045

GPS Coordinates: 47.43149° N, 121.77500° W

Did You Know? Between 1906 and 1915, the town of Moncton existed on the northern shore of Rattlesnake Lake, but it was destroyed by flooding from Chester Morse Lake, which drained into Rattlesnake Lake.

Rattlesnake Mountain Scenic Area

The Rattlesnake Mountain Scenic Area covers 1,851 acres of the southern mountainous ridge of the Snoqualmie Valley. Here, you can find Douglas fir forests, pockets of old-growth forests, cliffs, and steep slopes.

This area is also home to a wide array of wildlife, including northern spotted owls, peregrine falcons, blacktail deer, Roosevelt elk, black bears, cougars, bobcats, coyotes, foxes, and ospreys. This lovely part of the state offers some of the most scenic hiking in the Cascade foothills.

The ridge's 10-mile trail provides views of Mount Si, the upper Snoqualmie Valley, and the Cascades. At the south end, you'll be rewarded with a fantastic view of the Cedar River Watershed from the 1,000-foot-tall ledges above Rattlesnake Lake.

Best Time to Visit: Year round, though trails are sometimes snowy in winter

Closest City or Town: North Bend

Physical Address: 37580 Winery Rd, Snoqualmie, WA 98065

GPS Coordinates: 47.4308° N, 121.7751° W

Did You Know? Rattlesnake Lake received its name around 1850 from Seattle pioneer Arthur A. Denny. The sound of the wind rattling camas seed pods was mistaken as a rattlesnake by a scared road surveyor from Denny's group. Little did he know, there are no venomous snakes in Western Washington.

Drumheller Channels National Natural Landmark

Drumheller Channels National Natural Landmark is an example of Channeled Scablands. This may be in the same state as Western Washington's evergreen forests and snowy-peaked mountains, but it seems like an entirely different world. The scablands are comprised of strange rocky land formations and barren bedrock. Formed from ice-age flooding, the bedrock is crisscrossed by coulees (long channels), which is where the Channeled Scablands got their name. With its fascinating landscape, this geological wonder is a fantastic area for a scenic drive.

There are also several great hikes you can take around the coulees. An easy hike around Twin Lakes will provide gorgeous views of lakes, marshes, and wetlands, as well as vibrant wildflowers and geese, ducks, bald eagles, and ospreys for birdwatchers.

Best Time to Visit: April through September

Closest City or Town: Odessa

Physical Address: W McManamon Rd, Othello, WA 99344

GPS Coordinates: 47.4042° N, 118.7439° W

Did You Know? The scablands were created 10,000 to 20,000 years ago by one of the biggest mega floods in world history.

Nisqually River

The glacial-fed Nisqually River starts on the southern slope of Mount Rainier and flows for 78 miles, eventually terminating in the Puget Sound. Moving down the river, you'll find a scenic landscape of forests, mountains, and rolling farmland.

The beautiful river is a popular destination for fishing enthusiasts. The river's waters are rich with rainbow and cutthroat trout, as well as various species of salmon. Swimming and boating are some other popular activities in the summer. Don't forget to check out the Nisqually River Water Trail, where you can float down the river on non-motorized watercraft and take in the gorgeous views.

There are plenty of opportunities along the river for mountain biking, hiking, and horseback riding. For birdwatchers, the area is home to bald eagles, peregrine falcons, marbled murrelets, northern goshawks, pileated woodpeckers, and northern spotted owls.

Best Time to Visit: October for fishing

Closest City or Town: Ashford

Physical Address: 11642 6th Ave SE, Olympia, WA 98513

GPS Coordinates: 46.7408° N, 121.9177° W

Did You Know? In the U.S., the Nisqually River is the only river with headwaters in a national park and a delta in a national wildlife refuge.

Washington State Capitol Building

Located in Olympia, the capital of Washington, the Washington State Capitol Building was originally built in 1854 on 12 acres of land on a hill that overlooks what is now Capitol Lake.

At the time, Washington was still a territory. In 1889, with the approval of the state's admittance to the Union, President Benjamin Harrison donated 132,000 federal acres to build a new capitol for the new state.

After quite a bit of debate and wrangling, construction began on the building in 1912 and was fully completed in 1928. The main Legislative Building is the home of the statehouse and senate and features the tallest self-supporting masonry dome in the country.

Best Time to Visit: The Washington State Capitol Building is open Monday through Friday from 7:30 a.m. to 5:00 p.m. and weekends from 11:00 a.m. to 4:00 p.m.

Pass/Permit/Fees: There is no fee to visit the Washington State Capitol Building.

Closest City or Town: Olympia

Physical Address: 416 Sid Snyder Ave SW, Olympia, WA 98504

GPS Coordinates: 47.03664° N, 122.90436° W

Did You Know? As the oldest building on the capitol campus, the governor's mansion has served as the primary residence of Washington's governors since 1909.

82

White Bluffs

White Bluffs is a particularly striking part of the state that will give you a change of pace from the forests of the west. Also known as Hanford Reach, White Bluffs is full of sand dunes and high deserts with views of the Columbia River.

On the other side of the river, you can see the Hanford Campus, where there are reactors that date back to World War II. The rushing rivers and sands that surround you with the expansive sky above will make you feel truly at one with nature.

The area is also rich in wildlife. In the sand, you can find small mammals and lizards, while in the marshier areas, you might catch sight of ravens, ospreys, herons, red-winged blackbirds, and golden or bald eagles. While the White Bluffs South Slope Trail is rated as difficult, the White Bluffs North Slope Trail is appropriate for hikers at all levels of experience, including families.

Best Time to Visit: April through June and September

Closest City or Town: Othello

Physical Address: White Bluffs Trailhead, Ringold River Rd, Mesa, WA 99343

GPS Coordinates: 46.6772° N, 119.4446° W

Did You Know? Hundreds of years ago, Native American tribes used the White Bluffs area to cross the river and as a place to gather for celebrations and trading.

Goat Rocks Wilderness

The Goat Rocks Wilderness spreads across 108,023 acres between Mount Rainier and Mount Adams and provides beautiful views of Cascade peaks and volcanoes. The Goat Rocks that the wilderness surrounds are the ancient remains left behind from a volcano that existed 2 million years ago.

At 8,201 feet, Gilbert Peak is the highest point in the Goat Rock ranges. Below the ridges are alpine meadows filled with small glacial lakes and ponds. In this area, you might see marmots, pikas, deer, and elk.

The mountain goats for which the area is named are found at high elevations. The wilderness features 120 miles of trails. Many hikers believe that Goat Rocks is the most scenic area along the northern half of the 2,650-mile-long Pacific Crest Trail.

Best Time to Visit: Late July through October

Closest City or Town: Packwood

Physical Address: Goat Rocks Wilderness, Randle, WA 98377

GPS Coordinates: 46.6085° N, 121.6280° W

Did You Know? The Goat Rocks area features four major glaciers: McCall, Packwood, Meade, and Conrad.

Palouse Falls State Park

Palouse Falls State Park is a must-see for fans of ice-age floods. Palouse Falls was carved over 13,000 years ago and is one of the last active waterfalls on the flood path. The waterfall is 198 feet tall and surrounded by basalt cliffs.

The place is a paradise for photographers and painters—the glorious falls rushing down in the changing light are a sight that just begs to be documented. There are three different viewpoints from which you can see the falls. The lowest view is the most direct, while the second features an interpretive path with facts about the canyon.

Fryxell Overlook is the highest viewpoint, and from here, you can see marvelous panoramic views of Palouse River Canyon and the falls. The surrounding park is a popular location for picnicking and birdwatching.

Best Time to Visit: Sunset, year round

Closest City or Town: Perry

Physical Address: Palouse Falls Rd, LaCrosse, WA 99143

GPS Coordinates: 46.6638° N, 118.2273° W

Did You Know? Palouse Falls was designated Washington's state waterfall in 2014. The bill advocating for the designation was written by local schoolchildren.

Enchanted Valley

The Enchanted Valley is located deep in the Olympic Mountains with trails that lead visitors through old-growth forests and meadows of wildflowers.

First popularized in the 1930s, the Enchanted Valley was initially a horseback-riding and hiking retreat, and Tom E. Criswell built a chalet in 1931 for overnight guests.

The retreat was in operation until the mid-1980s before the chalet was boarded up. It is still on the property but sits unused. However, the trails are still extremely popular for day and overnight hikes.

Best Time to Visit: The best time to visit the Enchanted Valley is during the summer.

Pass/Permit/Fees: There is a fee of $30 per vehicle to visit the Olympic National Park, where the Enchanted Valley is located. For backpacking the trails, you'll need to register for an overnight permit. Permit information is found on the park website.

Closest City or Town: Port Angeles

Physical Address: Graves Creek Trailhead, Graves Creek Rd, Quinault, WA 98575

GPS Coordinates: 47.66962° N, 123.39500° W

Did You Know? The Enchanted Valley is referred to as "the valley of 10,000 waterfalls" by locals.

Olympic National Park

Olympic National Park spans nearly 1 million acres and features a uniquely diverse landscape. Here, you'll find old-growth rainforests, glaciated mountains, and more than 75 miles of the Pacific Coast. The list of outdoor recreational activities available in the park is nearly endless. You can explore tidepools, go boating, backpack into the wilderness, and more. The area is excellent for fishing salmon, trout, and char.

The park also features a whopping 16 campgrounds. At night, you can gaze up at the spectacular night sky, unmarred by human-made light. Rangers regularly lead interpretive walks and campfire programs, as well as snowshoe walks at Hurricane Ridge in the winter. This park is a hiker's heaven with trails through temperate rainforests, mountains, lowland forests, and along the coast.

Best Time to Visit: The park is open year round with many winter activities. However, the rainforests can get up to 50 inches of rain in the winter, so the best time to visit them is spring through fall.

Closest City or Town: Port Angeles

Physical Address: 3002 Mt Angeles Rd, Port Angeles, WA 98362

GPS Coordinates: 48.0993° N, 123.4257° W

Did You Know? The park was originally dubbed the Mount Olympus National Monument by President Theodore Roosevelt in 1909.

Port Angeles

Originally named Puerto de Nuestra Senora de los Angeles
("Port of our Lady of the Angels") by Francisco de Eliza, a
Spanish Explorer who was one of the first Europeans in the
area in 1791, Port Angeles received its shorter name by
English-speaking settlers in the mid-1800s.

In 1890, Port Angeles was called the "Second National
City," as it was one of just two cities in the United States
officially developed by the federal government
(Washington D.C. being the other).

Best Time to Visit: The most ideal time to visit Port
Angeles is during the summer for the best weather.

Pass/Permit/Fees: There is no fee to visit Port Angeles,
but individual activities may have separate charges.

Closest City or Town: Port Angeles

Physical Address: Port Angeles Visitor Center, 121 E
Railroad Ave, Port Angeles, WA 98362

GPS Coordinates: 48.12614° N, -123.43155° W

Did You Know? Today, Port Angeles is known as the
"Gateway to the Olympic National Park," and its unique
position as a seaside and mountain town makes it a popular
destination for vacationers.

Sol Duc Falls Trail

Located in Olympic National Park, Sol Duc Falls Trail is a favorite natural attraction because of its towering trees, alpine lakes, cascading falls, and snowcapped peaks. The trailhead to Sol Duc Falls begins just beyond the Sol Duc Hot Springs and Resort, which was once the home of the Sol Duc Hotel, built in 1912.

While this five-star hotel drew massive crowds and rave reviews, it was unfortunately destroyed by fire in 1920. Along the family-friendly and relatively flat trail to the falls, you'll pass under a dense forest canopy, cross a small stream on a bridge, and watch the water flow rapidly over mossy rocks. You'll hear the falls long before you see them, but they are just 0.8 miles from the trailhead.

Best Time to Visit: The best time to visit Sol Duc Falls is during the spring or summer after heavy rain.

Pass/Permit/Fees: There is a $25-per-vehicle fee to enter Olympic National Park.

Closest City or Town: Port Angeles

Physical Address: Sol Duc Trailhead, Sol Duc Rd, Port Angeles, WA 98363

GPS Coordinates: 47.95214° N, 123.81979° W

Did You Know? Sol Duc Falls cascades 48 feet down the rocky canyon and splits into as many as four channels on its way down.

Port Townsend

A perfect blend of yesterday and today, Port Townsend combines the charm of the Victorian Era with the modernity of activities like whale-watching tours, a maritime center, and the Marine Science Center. Beaches, boats, and boutiques are readily available in Port Townsend, a town that dates from the 1800s.

Be sure to visit some of the numerous museums in the restored downtown area, including Kelly's Art Deco Lighting Museum, the Jefferson Museum of Art and History, the Puget Sound Coast Artillery Museum, and the Port Townsend Aero Museum, among others. There are also two historic theaters (The Uptown and the Rose Theatre) for nighttime fun after you've spent the day in the fresh air of the beach.

Best Time to Visit: The best time to visit Port Townsend is during the summer when the water is warmest.

Pass/Permit/Fees: There is no fee to visit Port Townsend.

Closest City or Town: Port Townsend

Physical Address: Port Townsend Visitor Information Center, 2409 Jefferson St, Port Townsend, WA 98368

GPS Coordinates: 48.12360° N, 122.78981° W

Did You Know? Port Townsend is one of the driest towns in Washington, as it is in the "Rain Shadow" region by the Olympic Mountains. It only receives 19 inches of rain per year.

Poulsbo

Poulsbo is located on Kitsap Peninsula and is a popular destination for visitors who want to explore "Little Norway." The galleries, specialty shops, and museums in the downtown area of Poulsbo provide endless opportunities to enjoy a charming European-style town with a scenic view of the ocean.

At just 4.5 square miles, Poulsbo features views of Liberty Bay and the Olympic Mountains in the west. The original Scandinavian settlers chose this area because of its similarities to Norwegian fjords, but before they arrived, the area was home to the Suquamish Native American tribe who had lived in the region for thousands of years.

Best Time to Visit: The best time to visit Poulsbo is during the summer when the weather is warmer.

Pass/Permit/Fees: There is no fee to visit Poulsbo.

Closest City or Town: Poulsbo

Physical Address: Poulsbo Visitor's Center, 19010 Front St NE, Poulsbo, WA 98370

GPS Coordinates: 47.7384° N, 122.6197° W

Did You Know? Poulsbo was founded by Jorgen Eliason, who hailed from Fordefjord, Norway.

Jade Lake

This gorgeous lake located in the Alpine Lakes Wilderness is named for its incredibly blue waters that originate at Lynch Glacier. It is one of the dozens of lakes in the Central Cascades Mountains that are accessible by trails of various grades. The hiking paths that lead to Jade Lake also connect to Marmot and Clarice lakes in the same area.

The trail to Jade and Marmot lakes is one of the longer ones at 20 miles in length. Marmot Lake will be the first one you pass about 4 miles into the hike.The water in all three lakes is cold, but if you want to take a dip, you're more than welcome. Otherwise, you'll enjoy the scenic waterfalls, cliffs, and vegetation surrounding the beautiful waters.

Best Time to Visit: The best time to visit Jade Lake is in the summer, especially if you want to go in the water.

Pass/Permit/Fees: An annual Northwest Forest Pass is $30, and a single-day pass to Jade Lake is $5.

Closest City or Town: Roslyn

Physical Address: Tucquala Meadows Trailhead, N-F Rd 4330, Ronald WA 98940

GPS Coordinates: 47.5978° N, 121.1806° W

Did You Know? The hike to Jade Lake is rated as difficult and requires off-trail hiking, multiple river crossings, and steep inclines. You may need to trek through snow, even in the summer.

Friday Harbor

Known as the "Gateway to the San Juan Islands," Friday Harbor is a walkable seaport with historic buildings, friendly shops, and award-winning restaurants. Located just a few feet from the ferry landing, you won't have to go far to experience a true San Juan vacation. The Whale Museum, the San Juan Community Theatre, the San Juan Historical Museum, and the San Juan Islands Museum of Art are all within walking distance of the ferry landing, making it simple to pick and choose exactly what you want to see and do at a moment's notice. You can also take an inter-island ferry to the Shaw, Orcas, and Lopez islands from Friday Harbor.

Best Time to Visit: The best time to visit Friday Harbor is during the summer when the weather is more predictable.

Pass/Permit/Fees: There is no fee to visit Friday Harbor itself, but there is a fee to take the Washington State Ferry or other transportation to the San Juan Islands.

Closest City or Town: Seattle

Physical Address: The Whale Museum, 62 First St N, Friday Harbor, WA 98250

San Juan Historical Museum, 405 Price St, Friday Harbor, WA 98250

GPS Coordinates: 48.5387°N, 123.0174° W

Did You Know? Friday Harbor was founded in 1845 when the Hudson's Bay Company claimed San Juan Island.

Kerry Park

This small 1.26-acre park located on Queen Ann Hill in Seattle overlooks downtown and is considered to have one of the best views of Seattle's skyline. The Space Needle is centered with Elliott Bay to the west and Mount Rainier providing a picturesque backdrop.

There are few amenities in this park, with just a railing and several park benches facing the skyline view, but it does include a steel sculpture called *Changing Form* by artist Doris Totten Chase.

This 15-foot-tall statue was built in 1971 and is a popular subject for photographers. There is also a small playground on site for children.

Best Time to Visit: The best time to visit Kerry Park is on clear days when the skyline is most visible.

Pass/Permit/Fees:
There is no fee to visit Kerry Park.

Closest City or Town: Seattle

Physical Address: 211 W Highland Dr, Seattle, WA 98119

GPS Coordinates: 47.63039° N, 122.36005° W

Did You Know? Kerry Park is named for Albert S. and Katharine Kerry, who lived near the land and donated it to Seattle in 1927 "so that all who stop here may enjoy [the] view."

Lake Union

A substantial part of the Washington Ship Canal, Lake Union is a freshwater lake that is situated entirely in the city of Seattle. The Ship Canal Bridge is to the east, and the George Washington Memorial Bridge is to the west.

The lake was naturally formed 12,000 years ago by the Vashon glacier, which is also responsible for forming Lake Washington, Green Lake, Bitter Lake, and Haller Lake.

Many surrounding Seattle neighborhoods are named for their position relative to the lake, including Westlake, Northlake, Eastlake, and South Lake Union. The lake is popular for fishing, boating, and community events.

Best Time to Visit: The best time to visit Lake Union is during the summer.

Pass/Permit/Fees: There is no fee to visit Lake Union.

Closest City or Town: Seattle

Physical Address: 860 Terry Ave N, Seattle, WA 98109

GPS Coordinates: 47.6423° N, 122.3326° W

Did You Know? The name Lake Union comes from a prediction by Thomas Mercer, who said in 1854 that the canals would eventually connect Lake Washington and Puget Sound in a "union of waters." Originally, it was known as *Lushootseed* or "small lake" by the Duwamish, who were comparing it to Lake Washington.

Olympic Sculpture Park

A 9-acre outdoor sculpture museum, the Olympic Sculpture Park is located on the waterfront just 1 mile north of the Seattle Art Museum. There are several permanent sculptures and site-specific installations, along with a rotating exhibition that features major artists such as Spencer Finch, Victoria Haven, and Regina Silveira.

The sculpture park was formerly an industrial site that belonged to Unocal until the 1970s. The idea to turn the contaminated brownfield into an art park was conceived in 1996 and realized in 2007 with a $30 million donation from Mary and Jon Shirley.

Best Time to Visit: The best time to visit the Olympic Sculpture Park is during the spring, summer, or fall when the weather is warmer.

Pass/Permit/Fees: There is no fee to visit the Olympic Sculpture Park.

Closest City or Town: Seattle

Physical Address: 2901 Western Ave, Seattle, WA 98121

GPS Coordinates: 47.61724° N, 122.35527° W

Did You Know? Despite community objections, the Waterfront Streetcar was demolished to create space for the Olympic Sculpture Park.

Pike Place Market

Pike Place Market is a lively community in the center of downtown Seattle that's comprised of hundreds of small businesses, farmers, crafters, and residents. There are numerous historic buildings in the area, which were saved 50 years ago when the Seattle electorate chose to preserve the market from demolition.

It is the one place in town where you can meet the person responsible for growing, making, or raising your products. In 1964, the Friends of the Market nonprofit group was established to save the market from the wrecking ball. Today, you'll find a farmers market, a crafts market, and a specialty foods market that each sells locally produced goods and unique gifts.

Best Time to Visit: Produce stands and farm tables are open daily from 9:00 a.m. to 5:00 p.m., and fish markets are open daily from 9:00 a.m. to 4:00 p.m. The Crafts Market is open daily from 10:00 a.m. to 5:00 p.m.

Pass/Permit/Fees: There is no fee to visit Pike Place Market but bring money for shopping!

Closest City or Town: Seattle

Physical Address: 85 Pike St, Seattle, WA 98101

GPS Coordinates: 47.6092° N, 122.3406° W

Did You Know? Pike Place Market is world famous for its "flying fish," where fish mongers shout orders and toss their fish to each other and paying customers.

Seattle Aquarium

The Seattle Aquarium, which was established in 1977, is considered a model facility, and its design has been adopted by many leading zoos and aquariums in the United States. Three decades after its opening, the aquarium added 18,000 square feet of space for a 120,000-gallon exhibit, a café, a meeting and event space, a gift shop, and more. There are currently six major exhibits to explore in the aquarium, which are *Window on Washington Waters*, *Pacific Coral Reef*, *Underwater Dome*, *Marine Mammals, Birds & Shores*, and *Life on the Edge*. By attendance, the Seattle Aquarium is the ninth-largest aquarium in the country.

Best Time to Visit: The Seattle Aquarium is open daily from 9:30 a.m. to 6:00 p.m., with the last entry at 5:00 p.m.

Pass/Permit/Fees: The fee to visit the Seattle Aquarium ranges from $20.95 to $29.95 for adults and from $18.20 to $23.20 for children between the ages of 4 and 12 depending on the day you visit.

Closest City or Town: Seattle

Physical Address: 1483 Alaskan Way Pier 59, Seattle, WA 98101

GPS Coordinates: 47.6082° N, 122.3429° W

Did You Know? Since the Seattle Aquarium opened in 1977, more than 27 million people have visited its exhibits, and more than 2 million schoolchildren have received marine conservation education through the aquarium's programs.

Seattle Ferry Terminal

Known as either Pier 52 or Colman Dock, the primary ferry terminal in Seattle is operated by the Washington State Ferry System. Colman Dock has been in operation since 1882 and is named for the Scottish engineer James Colman, who built the original pier. Along with most of Seattle, Colman Dock burned to the ground during the Great Seattle Fire of 1889, but it was rebuilt and, in 1908, was even extended to 705 feet in length. Currently, two ferry routes, the Seattle-Bainbridge ferry and the Seattle-Bremerton Ferry, depart from Colman Dock, but two passenger-only ferries operate from Pier 50 on the south side (Kitsap Fast Ferries and the King County Water Taxi).

Best Time to Visit: The best time to visit the Seattle Ferry Terminal is during the summer when the weather is warmer.

Pass/Permit/Fees: The fee to take the Seattle Ferry from Colman Dock or Pier 50 varies based on age, vehicle, and route. Check the website for specific costs.

Closest City or Town: Seattle

Physical Address: Pier 55, 1101 Alaskan Way, Seattle, WA 98101. This pier offers scenic views and is a six-minute walk from the ferry terminal.

GPS Coordinates: 47.6034° N, 122.3385° W

Did You Know? More than 4.5 million people travel between Seattle and Bainbridge Island on the Seattle–Bainbridge ferry each year, a trip that takes 35 minutes to complete.

The Museum of Flight

With more than 175 aircraft and spacecraft, tens of thousands of aviation artifacts, millions of photographs, and a first-class library, the Museum of Flight is the largest independent air and space museum in the world.

Established in 1965 when several aviation enthusiasts decided to save the numerous important aviation artifacts that were being lost or destroyed, the museum opened in the Seattle Center, where the 1962 World's Fair was held. Ten years later, the museum moved to the Boeing Red Barn, which has been leased to the museum for 99 years.

Best Time to Visit: The Museum of Flight is open daily from 10:00 a.m. to 5:00 p.m.

Pass/Permit/Fees: Adult admission is $25, and seniors ages 65 and over are $21. Children between the ages of 5 and 17 are $17, and children ages 4 and under are free.

Closest City or Town: Seattle

Physical Address: 9404 E Marginal Way S, Seattle, WA 98108

GPS Coordinates: 47.5190° N, 122.2969° W

Did You Know? In 2002, the Library and Archives Building was added to the Museum of Flight, and in 2004, the J. Elroy McCaw Personal Courage Wing and Airpark joined as well.

The Showbox

The Showbox opened its doors in 1939 and has been entertaining audiences for over 80 years. It is one of the city's few venues that has provided music enthusiasts in Seattle with an incredible range of entertainment from the Jazz Age to folk music, the Grunge Era to the current hip hop and neo-folk music of today.

The Showbox has hosted numerous big-name musicians such as Duke Ellington, the Ramones, Muddy Waters, Gypsy Rose Lee, Pearl Jam, Macklemore, Prince, The Roots, Foo Fighters, and many others.

Best Time to Visit: The best time to visit The Showbox is when a musical act you want to see is appearing on stage. Check the website for a schedule of upcoming appearances.

Pass/Permit/Fees: The fee to visit The Showbox depends on the show and seat selection.

Closest City or Town: Seattle

Physical Address: 1426 1st Ave, Seattle, WA 98101

GPS Coordinates: 47.6092° N, 122.3393° W

Did You Know? The Showbox was slated for demolition in 2019 but was saved through a petition with 110,000 signatures that sought to preserve the building as a historical site.

The Space Needle and Seattle Center

As one of the most recognized landmarks in the United States, if not the world, the Space Needle is the icon of Seattle. It was built for the 1962 World's Fair, which had the theme of *The Age of Space.* The Space Needle's structure symbolized the aspirations of humanity concerning the Space Age. It is 605 feet tall and features a 520-foot flying saucer–shaped observation building at the top of the tower. Visitors to the top can take in the 360-degree view of downtown Seattle, Puget Sound, Mount Rainier, the Cascades, and the Olympic Mountains.

Best Time to Visit: The Space Needle and Seattle Center are open Sunday, Monday, and Thursday from 9:30 a.m. to 9:00 p.m., Tuesday and Wednesday from 9:30 a.m. to 8:00 p.m., and Friday and Saturday from 9:30 a.m. to 9:30 p.m.

Pass/Permit/Fees: The fee to visit the Space Needle depends on the day. Adult admission is between $34 and $37.50, and senior admission (65+) is between $29 and $32.50. Youth admission (between ages 5 and 12) is between $25 and $30.

Closest City or Town: Seattle

Physical Address: 400 Broad St, Seattle, WA 98109

GPS Coordinates: 47.6212° N, 122.3492° W

Did You Know? The Loupe, which was part of a 2018 renovation, gives visitors to the Space Needle a downward view of the structure and surrounding area. It's the only rotating glass floor in the world.

Woodland Park Zoo

The Woodland Park Zoo was established in 1899. Since then, it's catered to 1 million visitors each year. Founded by Englishman Guy Phinney, the Woodland Park Zoo got its start as a formal rose garden and deer park. Eventually, the city purchased Woodland Park and created a small zoo from the collection of animals once owned by the Lake Washington Cable Railway.

After undergoing several renovations and additions throughout the years, the most recent campaign occurred in 1985, when the *Asian Elephant Forest*, *Tropical Rain Forest*, *Northern Trail*, and *Trail of Vines* exhibits were added.

Best Time to Visit: The Woodland Park Zoo is open daily from 9:30 a.m. to 4:00 p.m. Hours may be extended in the summer.

Pass/Permit/Fees: Adult admission is $24.60. Children between the ages of 3 and 12 are $15, and children under the age of 3 are free. Seniors ages 65 and older are $22.60.

Closest City or Town: Seattle

Physical Address: 5500 Phinney Ave N, Seattle, WA 98103

GPS Coordinates: 47.6692° N, 122.3508° W

Did You Know? The Woodland Park Zoo founder, Guy Phinney, invested $40,000 of his own money to build a park on his land near Greenlake.

North Cascades National Park

North Cascades National Park was founded in 1968 to preserve the area's gorgeous mountains, forests, subalpine meadows, plentiful glaciers, and wildlife. The mountains are a great attraction for mountaineers and hikers, and some call them the "American Alps" due to their snow-covered tops.

With names like Mount Despair and Desolation Peak, the mountains may seem intimidating, but you'll feel nothing but awe-inspiring joy when you reach their magnificent peaks. There are countless wonders to experience in North Cascades National Park, but one you should be sure not to miss is Diablo Lake Overlook.

Diablo is a man-made reservoir with turquoise waters. The water gets its color from glacier-ground rock silt carried down by streams from the surrounding mountains. You'll be sure to want to snap a few photos, so don't forget your camera!

Best Time to Visit: Mid-June through late September

Closest City or Town: Sedro-Woolley

Physical Address: North Cascades National Park, State Rte 20 W, Sedro-Woolley, WA 98284

GPS Coordinates: 48.5384° N, 121.4481° W

Did You Know? Humans continually lived in the North Cascades National Park region for as long as 10,000 years.

Dungeness National Wildlife Refuge

With over 250 species of birds residing here, Dungeness National Wildlife Refuge is an absolute paradise for birdwatchers. Dungeness Spit is one of the longest natural sand spits on Earth. Here, you'll find a bay, mudflats, and sandy gravel beaches. But this area isn't without the state's signature lush forest trees as well.

This place is a haven of tranquility for wildlife that need protection from pounding waves and fierce winds. Unsurprisingly, wildlife watching is a popular activity on the refuge, as are hiking and photography.

The hike to the spit's historic lighthouse is nice and flat for less experienced hikers. At the lighthouse, you'll get the chance to have a bite at one of the picnic tables and refill your water before you carry on your scenic journey.

Best Time to Visit: The best time to see the birds is during their spring and fall migrations.

Closest City or Town: Sequim

Physical Address: 554 Voice of America Rd W, Sequim, WA 98382

GPS Coordinates: 48.1412° N, 123.1886° W

Did You Know? In 1792, Captain George Vancouver named Dungeness Spit after a famous headland on the southern coast of Kent.

Sequim-Dungeness Valley

If you're looking for a town that doesn't get as much rain as the rest of Washington, look no further than the Sequim-Dungeness Valley, which sees an equal amount of annual rainfall as Los Angeles. The small-town feel of Sequim provides visitors with solitude, while the surrounding Dungeness Valley provides them with beauty.

Shopping in the local boutiques and galleries is a favorite pastime of visitors, but don't forget to take a short drive to take in the bountiful lavender farms that surround the town. Plenty of outdoor activities such as hiking, birdwatching, biking, and paddling are available as well, especially given its temperate climate.

Best Time to Visit: The best time to visit the Sequim-Dungeness Valley is in the spring, summer, or fall.

Pass/Permit/Fees: There is no fee to visit the Sequim-Dungeness Valley.

Closest City or Town: Sequim

Physical Address: Sequim Visitor Information Center, 1192 E Washington St, Sequim, WA 98382

GPS Coordinates: 48.1138° N, 123.1055° W

Did You Know? In 2017, Sequim was named the Best Northwest Small Town by *USA Today*. It was also called one of the best unsung beach towns in the west by *Sunset Magazine*.

Mount Sawyer

A hike up Mount Sawyer will reward you with vibrant views of wildflower meadows along the way with wild blueberries, huckleberries, and heather surrounding most of the trail.

From the top, you'll have a 360-degree view of the Cascade Mountains with Glacier Peak and Mount Baker to the north, Mount Baring to the west, and Mount Rainier to the south.

Once you've taken in the view, you can head down the main trail to Sawyer Pass. There, you can have lunch amid the heather and huckleberries. Be sure to wear bright colors and make some noise during your visit, as bears and cougars are known to inhabit the area.

Best Time to Visit: Any time of year is great to visit—winter for snowshoeing, spring for wildflowers, summer for berry picking, and autumn for colors.

Closest City or Town: Skykomish

Physical Address: Tonga Ridge Trailhead, Skykomish, WA 98288

GPS Coordinates: 47.6787° N, 121.2648° W

Did You Know? Mount Sawyer was named after George Sawyer, a Skykomish district ranger who spent his life keeping watch for forest fires until his death in 1930.

Scenic Hot Springs

Like many of the other most beautiful spots in Washington, Scenic Hot Springs is not for the faint of heart. To reach the pools, you have to hike up into the dense forest, and the trail is at an incline the entire way. But the chance to relax in a hot-spring tub amid a gorgeous forest and mountains is well worth the trouble.

After your uphill trek, you will be greeted by the sight of the Scenic Hot Springs. In the fresh air, amongst the trees of the forest, you can enjoy a hot soak in tubs full of natural, crystal-clear mineral water.

The unpleasant sulfur smell you may associate with hot springs is also completely absent here. Scenic Hot Springs has three hot spring tubs, and each tub fits three to four people. Clothing is optional, so keep that in mind before you visit.

Best Time to Visit: Year round

Closest City or Town: Skykomish

Physical Address: This trail is accessed via unnamed roads and is located on private property. Access the Scenic Hot Spring's website to make reservation and plan your trek.

GPS Coordinates: 47.7075° N, 121.1374° W

Did You Know? Scenic Hot Springs was originally called *Madison Hot Springs* and was built in the 1890s to accommodate those who took the train from Seattle to visit the mineral baths.

Centennial Trail

One of the most popular trails in the state, Centennial Trail spans 30 miles from Snohomish to the Skagit County line. It is a 10-foot-wide paved path that provides a smooth travel experience for hikers, cyclists, skaters, and walkers, and there is a 6-foot-wide parallel equestrian trail for horseback riders.

Along the way, there are picnic tables, park benches, and at the Machias Trailhead, there are shelters available for rent. The Centennial Trail has served as a conservation corridor, an alternative transportation route, and a recreational pathway since its development in 1989 during the state's centennial celebration. It currently connects Snohomish, Lake Stevens, and Arlington.

Best Time to Visit: The best time to visit Centennial Trail is during spring, summer, or fall.

Pass/Permit/Fees: There is no fee to visit Centennial Trail.

Closest City or Town: Snohomish

Physical Address: Maple Ave, Snohomish, WA 98290

GPS Coordinates: 47.6869° N, 117.4911° W

Did You Know? Over 400,000 people use the Centennial Trail for recreation and as a non-motorized transportation corridor each year.

Snoqualmie Falls

A glacier waterfall, Snoqualmie Falls was once a meeting and trading place for Native Americans in the Washington area. The Snoqualmie tribe established their camp at the base of nearby Mount Si and villages at Tolt and Fall City. When white settlers arrived near the falls in the 1850s, the waterfall became a favorite recreational area for the pioneers. Jeremiah Borst became the first permanent white settler in the valley and is sometimes called "the father of the Snoqualmie Valley." Due to the waterfall's height, it has attracted daredevils throughout the years, including Mr. Blondin walking a tightrope over the falls in 1889 and Charlie Anderson parachuting into the canyon from a hot air balloon in 1890. He did not survive this attempt.

Best Time to Visit: The best time to visit Snoqualmie Falls is during the spring or summer when the water is running at its best.

Pass/Permit/Fees: There is a $5 parking fee to visit Snoqualmie Falls.

Closest City or Town: Snoqualmie

Physical Address: 37451 SE Fish Hatchery Rd, Fall City, WA 98024

GPS Coordinates: 47.5423° N, 121.8380° W

Did You Know? Snoqualmie Falls is 268 feet high and once served several logging operations downriver by floating logs over the falls.

John A. Finch Arboretum

This 65-acre public arboretum is located in Spokane and provides a gorgeous landscape full of approximately 2,000 trees and shrubs. Among the species in the arboretum, visitors will find 65 groups of lilacs, a conifer grove, a maple grove, and a rhododendron grove. There's also a nature trail that winds along the Garden Springs Creek and planned seasonal activities throughout the year. Tours are also available during standard park hours, or feel free to explore the arboretum on your own. The Girl Scout Council in the Spokane area owns the Touch and See Nature Trail that is also located in the arboretum and was rehabilitated in 2004 by Darlea Chatburn, who earned her Gold Award for completing the project.

Best Time to Visit: The arboretum is open daily from dawn until dark.

Pass/Permit/Fees: There is no fee to visit the John A. Finch Arboretum.

Closest City or Town: Spokane

Physical Address: 3404 W Woodland Blvd, Spokane, WA 99224

GPS Coordinates: 47.6417° N, 117.4668° W

Did You Know? The John A. Finch Arboretum is named for an English settler who came to the United States and eventually moved to Spokane. He invested in numerous businesses in the area before passing away in 1915, leaving 40 percent of his estate to charity and civic organizations, including the arboretum.

Manito Park

Established in 1904, Manito Park has gone from an undeveloped recreational space with some picnic spots, a zoo, and several flower beds to a true community gathering place.

It features five major gardens (Rose Hill, Lilac Garden, Nishinomiya Tsutakawa Japanese Garden, Ferris Perennial Garden, and Duncan Garden), a pond, the Park Bench Café, the Gaiser Conservatory, and two large playgrounds for children. Canoes can now be rented onsite for visitors who want to relax on the pond.

Best Time to Visit: The best time to visit Manito Park is in the summer when the weather is warmer.

Pass/Permit/Fees: There is no fee to visit Manito Park.

Closest City or Town: Spokane

Physical Address: 1702 S Grand Blvd, Spokane, WA 99203

GPS Coordinates: 47.63939° N, 117.40978° W

Did You Know? Mirror Pond, which was once a natural lake called Mirror Lake, used to dry up during the summer. To prevent this, a concrete base was installed so that the water would be available year-round.

Martin Woldson Theater at The Fox

Originally constructed in 1931 and known as the Fox Theater, the Martin Woldson Theater at the Fox reopened its doors in 2007 to become the permanent home for the Spokane Symphony. In addition to symphony concerts and events, the theater also provides an Art Deco venue for various other artistic productions. When it initially opened, celebrities, movie stars, and 30,000 other people celebrated before viewing the world premiere of *Merely Mary Ann* on the movie screen. Artists such as Charles Farrell, Janet Gaynor, Will Rodgers, Anita Page, and Rosemarie enjoyed the Golden Jubilee grand opening.

Best Time to Visit: The best time to visit the Martin Woldson Theater at the Fox is when there is a performance on stage that you want to see. Check the website for dates and showtimes.

Pass/Permit/Fees: The fee to visit the Martin Woldson Theater at the Fox depends on the show and seat selection.

Closest City or Town: Spokane

Physical Address: 1001 W Sprague Ave, Spokane, WA 99201

GPS Coordinates: 47.6574° N, 117.4270° W

Did You Know? The Fox Theater was the first building in Spokane to be air conditioned. There were even picture windows that allowed visitors to peek into the mechanical room to see the air conditioning equipment.

Northwest Museum of Arts and Culture

As the largest cultural facility in the Inland Northwest, the Northwest Museum of Arts and Culture, or "MAC," hosts over 100,000 visitors a year. Since its inception in 1916, the museum has become one of five Smithsonian affiliates in Washington State. It's committed to preserving and cultivating the heritage of people who've lived in the Inland Northwest. It boasts the largest collection of Plateau Indian art in the world with over 1 million objects of cultural materials, documents, photographs, artifacts, and fine art. Researchers flock to the museum to explore the Joel E. Ferris Research Archives, which contain a vast collection of materials from the Americas, Asia, and Europe.

Best Time to Visit: The Northwest Museum of Arts and Culture is open Tuesday through Sunday from 10:00 a.m. to 5:00 p.m.

Pass/Permit/Fees: Adult admission is $6, and seniors ages 65 and older are $5. Children between the ages of 6 and 17 are $4.

Closest City or Town: Spokane

Physical Address: 2316 W 1st Ave, Spokane, WA 99201

GPS Coordinates: 47.6573° N, 117.4455° W

Did You Know? The Northwest Museum of Arts and Culture has sponsored and presented the city's annual ArtFest for 33 consecutive years.

Riverfront Park

This 100-acre urban park is a hub of activity in Spokane that just half a century ago was an abandoned railyard. In 1974, Riverfront Park hosted the World's Fair, and today, it's an oasis in the middle of downtown. The Spokane River flows through the park.

As it drops over two dams and a basalt rock ledge, it creates the largest urban waterfall in the United States. Among the attractions at the Riverfront Park are the SkyRide, Riverfront Rotary Fountain, Looff Carrousel, Clocktower, Garbage Goat, Bloomsday Sculptures, Pavilion, Childhood Express, and more.

Best Time to Visit: The best time to visit Riverfront Park is during summer when all attractions are open and entertainment is abundant.

Pass/Permit/Fees: There is no fee to visit Riverfront Park.

Closest City or Town: Spokane

Physical Address: 507 N Howard St, Spokane, WA 99201

GPS Coordinates: 47.6625° N, 117.4192° W

Did You Know? The Looff Carrousel is a hand-carved ride from 1909 that has been placed on the National Register of Historic Places. It has 54 horses, 2 Chinese dragons, 1 giraffe, and 1 tiger. Riders can grab a ring from a dispenser on each pass to toss at a clown target during the ride.

ROW Adventure Center

If you're looking for a guided outdoor adventure in the Spokane area, the ROW Adventure Center can deliver a unique, exciting experience for visitors of all ages. Choose from whitewater rafting down the Spokane River, kayaking in the Coeur d'Alene Lake, biking along the Trail of the Coeur d'Alene and Heyburn State Park, or fly fishing in St. Joe or Coeur d'Alene River. ROW Adventure Center's guiding mission is to provide safe, exhilarating opportunities to experience the incredible natural wonders in and around Spokane.

Best Time to Visit: The ROW Adventure Center is open Monday through Friday from 9:00 a.m. to 5:00 p.m., but adventures are scheduled based on availability. Contact the ROW Adventure Center directly to book your adventure.

Pass/Permit/Fees: The fee to visit the ROW Adventure Center will depend on the adventure you select.

Closest City or Town: Spokane

Physical Address: 209 S Washington St, Spokane, WA 99201

GPS Coordinates: 47.6547° N, 117.4176° W

Did You Know? ROW Adventure Center's parent company was founded in 1979 and since then has provided more than 200,000 guests with adventures they'll never forget.

St. John's Cathedral

When St. John's Cathedral underwent construction in 1925 and 1929, three parishes in Spokane (St. Peter's, St. James, and All Saints Cathedral) merged to become the Cathedral of St. John the Evangelist. The cathedral is constructed entirely of cut stone, and the stained glass and carvings include various symbols of several faiths. One of the most notable features of the cathedral is the Cathedral Organ, which has 4,039 pipes. It was installed in 1957 and renovated in 2000. In Bishop Cross Tower, a 49-bell carillon sounds during Sunday services and various religious and civic celebrations throughout the year.

Best Time to Visit: The cathedral can be toured by appointment, but you can also attend one of several worship services each week. There is an 8:00 a.m. Sunday service without music, a 10:30 a.m. Sunday service that features choral worship, and various weekday services as announced on their website.

Pass/Permit/Fees: There is no fee to visit St. John's Cathedral.

Closest City or Town: Spokane

Physical Address: 127 E 12th Ave, Spokane, WA 99202

GPS Coordinates: 47.6454° N, 117.4099° W

Did You Know? St. John's Cathedral represents the vision of Right Reverend Edward Makin Cross, the third Bishop of Spokane, and is one of the few remaining examples of classic Gothic architecture in the country.

Museum of Glass

The Museum of Glass is a contemporary art museum that celebrates glass and glassmaking. It is the biggest and most active museum glass studio on the West Coast. Established in 2002, the museum was built on a Superfund site that initiated the restoration of the Thea Foss Waterway.

Visitors to the museum are treated to live glassmaking demonstrations, glass art exhibits, and the opportunity to attempt glassmaking at a hands-on workshop. More than 100,000 guests visit the museum each year, and it continues to attract more interest all the time. Not only does the museum boast a growing permanent collection, but it also features several traveling exhibitions throughout the year.

Best Time to Visit: The Museum of Glass is open Wednesday through Sunday from 10:00 a.m. to 5:00 p.m.

Pass/Permit/Fees: Adult admission is $17, and seniors ages 62 and older are $14. Children ages 6 through 12 are $5. Students and military members with ID are $14.

Closest City or Town: Tacoma

Physical Address: 1801 Dock St, Tacoma, WA 98402

GPS Coordinates: 47.2464° N, 122.4344° W

Did You Know? In 2017, *USA Today* named the Museum of Glass as one of the top ten tourist destinations in Washington State.

Puget Sound

Part of the Salish Sea (which consists of Puget Sound, the Strait of Georgia, and the Strait of Juan de Fuca) off the coast of the Pacific Northwest, Puget Sound is an inlet of the Pacific Ocean that extends approximately 100 miles from the northern point of Deception Pass to the southern point of Olympia.

Its maximum depth of 930 feet is off Jefferson Point, and its average depth is 450 feet. Puget Sound is also the name of the region that surrounds the body of water, which includes the major cities of Olympia, Everett, Tacoma, and Seattle. It is the second-largest estuary in the country, with the Chesapeake Bay in Maryland and Virginia taking the top spot.

Best Time to Visit: The most ideal time to visit Puget Sound is during the summer for the best weather.

Pass/Permit/Fees: There is no fee to visit Puget Sound, although various activities may require payment.

Closest City or Town: Tacoma

Physical Address: Browns Point Lighthouse Park, 201 Tulalip St NE, Tacoma, WA 98422

GPS Coordinates: 47.8000° N, 122.4522° W

Did You Know? Puget Sound is named in honor of Huguenot lieutenant Peter Puget, who accompanied George Vancouver on the Vancouver expedition in 1792.

Indian Heaven

Indian Heaven is a volcanic field surrounded by the 20,784-acre Indian Heaven Wilderness. At 5,927 feet, Lemei Rock is the highest point in the field. Lemei Rock's crater contains the picturesque Lake Wapiki.

This area is known for its colorful wildflowers in the summer. The wilderness is a high forested plateau with plentiful meadows and over 150 lakes. The lakes are great for fishing rainbow and brook trout.

With gorgeous colors, lush forests, and plentiful wildlife, this is a wonderful destination for hiking enthusiasts. On a hike, you may catch sight of a deer or elk and get the chance to snack on some ripe huckleberries. The area is also popular with bikers and horseback riders.

Best Time to Visit: Autumn for the fall colors

Closest City or Town: Trout Lake

Physical Address: Indian Heaven Wilderness, Gifford Pinchot, WA 98377

GPS Coordinates: 46.0480° N, 121.7546° W

Did You Know? The Wasco, Klickitat, Cascades, Umatilla, Yakama, and Wishram tribes gathered in the Indian Heaven area intermittently to fish, hunt, and pick berries over the past 9,000 years.

Cowiche Canyon

At just 3 miles in length, the Cowiche Canyon trail is one of the shorter ones included in this guide. However, there is a lot of beauty and wonder packed into this small package. You'll walk beneath spectacular andesite and basalt cliffs. The trail will also have you crossing Cowiche Creek several times along the way.

If you make your visit in the spring, gorgeous wildflowers will cover the hillsides. The beautiful chirps of songbirds will follow you through the whole hike as well. You may also be lucky enough to catch sight of a Lucia azure butterfly or a yellow-bellied marmot.

On the hike, there's a junction with the Winery Trail, which will take you to the Wilridge Vineyard and the Tasting Room of Yakima. If you like, you can take a little side trip to get some delicious wine with glorious views of Mount Adams.

Best Time to Visit: Spring for wildflowers, fall for color

Closest City or Town: Weikel

Physical Address: 8905 Scenic Dr, Yakima, WA 98908

GPS Coordinates: 46.6306 ° N, 120.6633° W

Did You Know? A railroad through the canyon was completed in 1923 and ran until 1984 when the line was abandoned. Alongside the trail, you may occasionally come across ties from the original railroad and even the remains of the old wagon trail that came before the rail line.

Okanogan-Wenatchee National Forest

Okanogan-Wenatchee National Forest is a vast and dynamic landscape, taking up 3.8 million acres along the eastern slopes of the Cascade Range. The forest is diverse, with tall, glaciated alpine peaks along the Cascade Crest, verdant valleys of ancient trees, and rugged shrub-steppe country at its eastern edge.

There are hundreds of miles of hiking trails through the wilderness and options to camp in developed campgrounds or out in the backcountry. This forest is a paradise when it comes to outdoor recreation—there's something for everyone.

You can hunt and fish to your heart's content. Or you can also go horseback riding, rock climbing, mountain biking, drive off-road vehicles, and more. In the winter, there's cross-country and downhill skiing, as well as snowmobiling. There are also Forest Service cabins available for rent.

Best Time to Visit: Year round

Closest City or Town: Winthrop

Physical Address: Okanogan-Wenatchee National Forest, Wenatchee, WA 98807

GPS Coordinates: 48.5190° N, 120.6744° W

Did You Know? The northern reaches of the Okanogan-Wenatchee are home to one of the largest populations of lynx in the lower 48 states.

Proper Planning

With this guide, you are well on your way to properly planning a marvelous adventure. When you plan your travels, you should become familiar with the area, save any maps to your phone for access without internet, and bring plenty of water—especially during the summer months. Depending on which adventure you choose, you will also want to bring snacks or even a lunch. For younger children, you should do your research and find destinations that best suit your family's needs. You should also plan when and where to get gas, local lodgings, and food. We've done our best to group these destinations based on nearby towns and cities to help make planning easier.

Dangerous Wildlife

There are several dangerous animals and insects you may encounter while hiking. With a good dose of caution and awareness, you can explore safely. Here are steps you can take to keep yourself and your loved ones safe from dangerous flora and fauna while exploring:

- Keep to the established trails.
- Do not look under rocks, leaves, or sticks.
- Keep hands and feet out of small crawl spaces, bushes, covered areas, or crevices.
- Wear long sleeves and pants to keep arms and legs protected.
- Keep your distance should you encounter any dangerous wildlife or plants.

Limited Cell Service

Do not rely on cell service for navigation or emergencies. Always have a map with you and let someone know where you are and how long you intend to be gone, just in case.

First Aid Information

Always travel with a first aid kit in case of emergencies.

Here are items you should be certain to include in your primary first aid kit:

- Nitrile gloves
- Blister care products
- Band-Aids in multiple sizes and waterproof type
- Ace wrap and athletic tape
- Alcohol wipes and antibiotic ointment
- Irrigation syringe
- Tweezers, nail clippers, trauma shears, safety pins
- Small zip-lock bags containing contaminated trash

It is recommended to also keep a secondary first aid kit, especially when hiking, for more serious injuries or medical emergencies. Items in this should include:

- Blood clotting sponges
- Sterile gauze pads
- Trauma pads

- Second-skin/burn treatment
- Triangular bandages/sling
- Butterfly strips
- Tincture of benzoin
- Medications (ibuprofen, acetaminophen, antihistamine, aspirin, etc.)
- Thermometer
- CPR mask
- Wilderness medicine handbook
- Antivenin

There is much more to explore, but this is a great start.

For information on all national parks, visit https://www.nps.gov/index.htm .

This site will give you information on up-to-date entrance fees and how to purchase a park pass for unlimited access to national and state parks. This site will also introduce you to all of the trails at each park.

Always check before you travel to destinations to make sure there are no closures. Some hiking trails close when there is heavy rain or snow in the area and other parks close parts of their land for the migration of wildlife. Attractions may change their hours or temporarily shut down for various reasons. Check the websites for the most up-to-date information.

Made in United States
Troutdale, OR
01/04/2024

16693621R00076